PHUKET & THE ANDAMAN COAST

SUZANNE NAM

Contents

Phuket & the Andaman Coast

Phuket

t's no wonder millions of people visit Phuket each year. If you're in the market for the perfect beach vacation and don't mind sharing your space with others, nothing can beat it. The landscape, with its hilly, green, forested interior and

clean, sandy beaches, is awe-inspiring. The vibes of the beaches and their surrounding areas vary from spring break fun to secluded romantic getaway to family-friendly. The accommodations range from unbelievably cheap to unbelievably luxurious. The tourism infrastructure is solid, and anything you want—perhaps a spur-of-the-moment diving trip, a midday massage on the beach, or a bespoke suit made in 24 hours—is available with no hassle. As if that weren't enough, nearly all of the sweeping, inviting beaches face west, so picture-perfect sunsets are a given. On an island this popular and this built-up, there are no more absolutely deserted places, but the northern and southern parts of the west coast offer some surprisingly quiet, quaint, and relaxed places to pull up a beach chair and chill out.

Thailand's largest island is about 48 kilometers (30 mi) long and 16 kilometers (10 mi) across. Imagine an elongated star with extra

points and you'll have a rough idea of what Phuket looks like from above. The points are promontories, rock formations jutting out into the ocean and separating the island into numerous individual beaches with curving coasts. The road system on the island is very well maintained, and there is both a coastal road that encircles nearly the whole island and large multilane inland roads. Off the main island, the Andaman Sea is littered with small islands and elegant rock formations jutting out from the sea. Many of the surrounding islands could be destinations in their own right, if not overshadowed by the main island.

Phuket and the surrounding areas rebuilt quickly after the 2004 tsunami, but the momentum from the redevelopment seems not to have slowed once all of the damage was repaired. There are new resorts and villas popping up in every corner, new shopping malls, bars and restaurants opening just off the beach and further inland, and more visitors

Previous: sunset on Phuket's west coast; Phuket Town. **Above:** monkeys on a beach in Phuket.

Look for ★ to find recommended
sights, activities, dining, and lodging.

Highlights

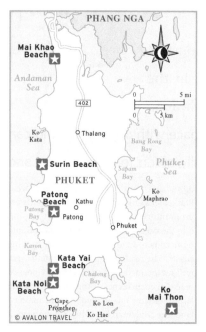

★ **Mai Khao Beach:** This quiet beach is fast becoming a favorite among families and local visitors, thanks to the ever-increasing selection of decent resorts and lack of crowds (page 12).

★ **Surin Beach:** This beautiful beach is quiet and relaxed, but offers plenty to do and great accommodations options (page 13).

★ **Patong Beach:** This busy, bustling beach is where you'll find all the action. Whether you're looking to shop, jet ski, parasail, or drink and dance the night away, you'll find it here (page 14).

★ **Kata Yai and Kata Noi Beaches:** These two beaches have clean, white sand and beautiful views, without the big crowds (page 14).

★ **Ko Mai Thon:** This little island is surrounded by stunning coral, making it a great place for snorkeling (page 18).

Phuket coastline

Phuket

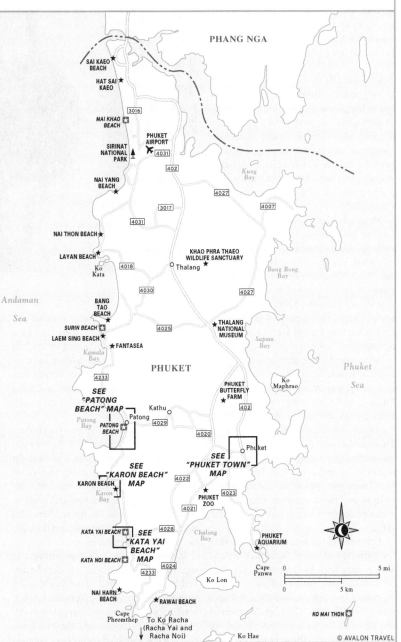

PHANG NGA

SAI KAEO BEACH

HAT SAI KAEO

3016

MAI KHAO BEACH

PHUKET AIRPORT

SIRINAT NATIONAL PARK

4031

402

Kung Bay

NAI YANG BEACH

4027

4007

3017

4031

NAI THON BEACH

LAYAN BEACH

Ko Kata

4018

KHAO PHRA THAEO WILDLIFE SANCTUARY

Thalang

Bang Rong Bay

Andaman Sea

4030

4027

BANG TAO BEACH

SURIN BEACH

LAEM SING BEACH

4025

THALANG NATIONAL MUSEUM

Sapam Bay

FANTASEA

Kamala Bay

PHUKET

Ko Maphrao

Phuket Sea

4233

SEE "PATONG BEACH" MAP

Kathu

PHUKET BUTTERFLY FARM

402

Patong Bay

Patong

PATONG BEACH

4029

4020

Phuket

SEE "PHUKET TOWN" MAP

SEE "KARON BEACH" MAP

KARON BEACH

Karon Bay

4022

4023

PHUKET ZOO

4021

KATA YAI BEACH

SEE "KATA YAI BEACH" MAP

4028

Chalong Bay

PHUKET AQUARIUM

KATA NOI BEACH

4024

4233

Ko Lon

Cape Panwa

0   5 mi

0   5 km

NAI HARN BEACH

RAWAI BEACH

Cape Phromthep   To Ko Racha
(Racha Yai and
Racha Noi)

Ko Hae

KO MAI THON

© AVALON TRAVEL

coming every year to stay, eat, drink, and shop in those new places. If you want to experience some of what Phuket became famous for, hurry up and come now: Even the most remote beaches and islands won't be the same in the next few years.

HISTORY

During prehistoric times, Phuket was inhabited by indigenous people sometimes referred to as Negritos, a group of hunter-gatherer pygmies who were, like many indigenous Southeast Asians, displaced and assimilated during waves of successive migration. Although no clear records exist, the last of the pygmy tribes was probably wiped out in the 19th century.

Although Phuket, then called Jang Si Lang or Junk Ceylon, shows up in some of Ptolemy's maps and writings, the island's history is largely unknown until about 800 years ago. Phuket's main natural resource, tin, was mined by prehistoric inhabitants, but what is now known as Phuket didn't come to the attention of the Thai people until the 13th century, when they arrived for trading and tin mining.

Word spread of the abundant natural resources, which included not only tin but also pearls, and by the 15th-16th centuries Thalang, as the island was then known, became a popular trading center, attracting the Dutch, Portuguese, and French. While Thailand has never technically been colonized, the Dutch set up trading posts in the region in the 16th century, and parts of the island were governed by tin traders under a concession. Phuket was even under the administration of the French between 1681 and 1685.

At the end of the Ayutthaya period, after the Burmese had sacked the capital city and were pushed back by General Taksin, they set their sights on Phuket and the surrounding region, invading the island and trying to take it over in 1785. The island's governor was killed by the intruders, but Phuket did not fall, according to the story told by nearly

rubber tapping

every islander. The governor's widow and her sister, both disguised as men, led a force against the siege and succeeded in repelling the Burmese after weeks of fighting. In recognition of their heroism, the two women were granted noble titles by King Rama I, and today there is a statue dedicated to them in the middle of the island.

After that dramatic high point in Phuket's history, the island continued to be used primarily as a tin-mining area, and later for rubber plantations, attracting thousands of Chinese immigrants in the 19th century, many of whom remained and, with the Muslim fisherfolk who immigrated from what is now Malaysia, constitute much of the modern indigenous population.

It wasn't until the 1970s that intrepid foreign travelers "discovered" Phuket's beauty and began to visit the island to enjoy the mountainous rainforests and pristine beaches. Starting with some small bungalow developments on Patong Beach, the island has boomed into a world-class tourist destination over the past three decades. Urban Thais in their 50s and 60s will often laugh and reminisce about what the Andaman coast used to be like before travelers and developers realized it was a natural tourist destination, when they'd head down on motorcycles to the largely untouched island for some adventure. Fast-forward 30 years, and the dirt roads and simple local folks have since been replaced by an exceptionally sophisticated infrastructure with easily navigable roads, hospitals, shopping malls, and an international airport.

Nowadays Phuket's "local" population is not just the Chinese immigrants and Muslim fisherfolk but thousands of Thais who've moved here to open hotels, restaurants, and other tourism-related businesses. The mining industry is virtually gone, but rubber tapping remains one of the island's income generators. The island's identity is tourism, attracting millions of visitors each year and accounting for the majority of the island's revenues.

PLANNING YOUR TIME

Phuket is filled with opportunities to relax on beautiful beaches, explore the stunning physical landscape, enjoy local foods, and pamper yourself in a bit of luxury. You can spend three weeks island-hopping, diving, hiking, and playing golf, or spend just a few days lying on the beach without even touring the neighboring areas, and you'll still have something of value from your trip.

While it may be tempting to idle your days away in the immediate vicinity of your hotel, make sure to set aside at least one day to explore the surrounding islands by boat. The small islands you'll pass on the way create scenery that's enchanting and like nothing in North America. Off the smaller islands is some of the best scuba and snorkeling in the world.

If you've never dived before, Phuket is the place to start. There are numerous dive schools that offer PADI certification, and the courses are inexpensive and a lot of fun. Even if you're not interested in diving, set aside a couple of hours to snorkel above some of the shallow coral reefs.

ORIENTATION

Patong functions as the center of the most popular and developed part of Phuket, though it's not in the middle of the island, but farther south. The northernmost part of the island, once almost totally ignored, is slowly becoming developed.

Beaches and Islands

While there are plenty of other sights that can fill your day, Phuket really is all about hanging out on the beaches and exploring the surrounding islands. Phuket is ringed with beaches, each with its own distinct personality. If you don't like one, go up a kilometer or two to the next one to find your perfect spot. Almost all of the sandy beaches on the island face west and look out onto the clear blue Andaman Sea, they are all clean, and they all offer at least minimum amenities (restrooms and small shops or food vendors for drinks and snacks) close by. Due to the island's topography, most of the beaches are separated from each other by rocky outcroppings, creating a natural curving bay at each. What really sets the beaches apart aside from size is what's going on behind them. A cozy beach chair with a great view will feel a lot different depending on whether there are copses of pine and palm trees behind you or a big street lined with shops, cafés, and restaurants. Luckily, whether you're looking for some action or just want peace and quiet, Phuket has both.

For most people, it's a good idea to pick the beach first, then the accommodations. Phuket has a main road running down the west coast, making all beaches easily accessible by car or scooter. On the island, the *sabai sabai* attitude tends to take hold quickly, and although all of the beaches are easy to access, it's a lot nicer to be able to walk to your favorite spot in a few minutes instead of taking a taxi or driving.

SAI KAEO BEACH
หาดทรายแก้ว

The northernmost beach on the island, Sai Kaeo Beach is one of the least developed and least populated, with just a few casual shacks selling seafood on the southern part of the beach and no hotels or other commercial enterprises to speak of. The golden coarse sand beach is backed by pine trees and gently curves before becoming Mai Khao to the south.

★ MAI KHAO BEACH
หาดไม้ขาว

Just below Sai Kaeo Beach is Mai Khao Beach, home to endangered giant leatherback turtles that lay their eggs in the sand during the cool season. When they hatch a few months later, usually in April, the babies make their way to the ocean en masse, a fascinating spectacle if you happen to be around when it happens. In recent years, community groups have beefed up protection of the turtles, restricting access to the beach during nesting and hatching periods. Although much of it is still a part of the national park and therefore undeveloped, not all is protected. There are a handful of resorts on this stretch of beach, although accommodations are spread out and options are limited. There are two coral reefs 1.5 kilometers (1 mi) out that can easily be seen with just a snorkel.

NAI YANG BEACH
หาดในยาง

Just south of the airport and Sirinat National Park is Nai Yang Beach, a small, gently curving bay with golden sand and surrounding pine and palm trees. Like other northern beaches, there is no large access road running parallel to the coast (the main road is inland about a quarter of a mile), so it is still relatively undeveloped and feels a little out of the way. There are a handful of resorts within walking distance of the beach, though so far nowhere right on the water.

NAI THON BEACH
หาดในทอน

This half-mile stretch of coastline, called Nai Thon Beach, is surrounded on either side by rocky promontories and forested hills. It has a

Mai Khao Beach

wide beach area covered in soft, light-colored sand. Though there are a few mostly high-end resorts on Nai Thon, even during high season it is a very quiet beach. No Jet Skis or parasails, but you can rent a beach chair with umbrella, and there are places to eat and drink along the beach.

LAYAN BEACH
หาดลายัน

Layan Beach, really just the northern tip of Bang Tao Beach, is small and quiet. During the April-October low season, this pristine beach is nearly deserted, and it may be as close to the desert-island experience as you'll find on Phuket. There's really nothing in the area aside from a couple of simple beachfront restaurants serving local food. Behind the beach is a more residential area, although there are numerous villas being built in the vicinity.

BANG TAO BEACH
หาดบางเทา

South of the airport but north of Patong and the island's central beaches is Bang Tao Beach, the longest beach on Phuket. Lagoons, resort and villa developments on the beach, and a main road far from the water make this a relatively quiet and uncrowded beach,

though it does have its share of touts and Jet Skis. The largest group of resorts is in a development called Laguna, which has seven different resorts spread out over 1,000 acres. Those resorts and the shared grounds take up most of the central part of Bang Tao Beach.

★ SURIN BEACH
หาดสุรินทร์

The perfect balance of secluded and interesting, Surin Beach has plenty to do, but none of the fast-paced activity you'll find on other popular beaches. The small, clean beach is backed by large green lawns and tall trees with only a small road behind it. Although there's no boardwalk, a pedestrian lane between the palms and pine trees is lined with small beach shops and restaurants, many of which set up dining areas right at the edge of the sand. Surrounding the beach area are some nice modern luxury resorts and some good dining options.

What makes Surin special is that it still feels like a local family beach, and it still feels like Thailand. There's a small town-meets-Miami Beach vibe here—local school kids playing volleyball on the lawn behind you while you sip a glass of wine on a comfy beach chair and watch the sun set. Surin is small, though,

Nai Thon Beach

and if you're looking for a place where you can wander around on foot for more than a few minutes, you will be disappointed here. The main road that runs perpendicular to the beach is too busy and fast to allow for much pedestrian activity, and there isn't much to see or do aside from right in the center near the beach anyway.

LAEM SING BEACH
หาดแหลมสิงห์

Tiny Laem Sing Beach was once a bit of a secret but is now a little more crowded and popular. It feels worlds away from the bustle of the area's other beaches. To access the small, curved beach, you'll have to walk down a steep path, and the shore is hidden from the main road. There are still some vendors selling fruit, snacks, and random souvenirs at Laem Sing, places to rent chairs, and even a few casual shops to grab lunch, so don't worry about amenities. Laem Sing also has some granite rock formations along the shore, making it a nice place to do a little casual snorkeling.

KAMALA BAY
อ่าวกมลา

Not quite like Karon or Kata to the south, but with a little more going on than Surin, the relatively undeveloped stretch of wide Kamala Bay, shaded by trees, is pleasant and relaxed. There are a few larger resorts right on the beach, and in the hills above the bay are a handful of small upscale hotels. Part of the beach is bordered by protected lands. Right behind the southern part of Kamala Bay is Kamala Village, a former fishing village that is still home to some who ply the ocean in their colorful longtail boats. The village isn't large but has a number of inexpensive guesthouses and places to get fresh seafood and other meals.

★ PATONG BEACH
หาดป่าตอง

Not quite the desert-island paradise you may have imagined, Patong Beach is a built-up, bustling beach community filled with Starbucks, McDonald's, scores of hotels and restaurants, a full-fledged shopping mall within walking distance of the beach, and a vibrant nightlife scene. For some, Patong is the only place to go in Phuket; for others, it's the worst-case scenario for a tropical vacation. If going out 'til the wee hours of the morning then rolling onto the beach to sleep it off with your fellow revelers is your thing, pick Patong. If you're looking for a quiet place to relax away from the hustle and bustle of urban life, stay away. The white-sand beach is generally covered with beach chairs and umbrellas by day but, despite being crowded, is a wide, clean beach with soft sand and clear water. It is one of the island's nicest beaches, if you don't mind lots of people or Jet Skis. The beach is one of the largest in the area, and the wide sidewalk has some small playgrounds and some interesting sculptures, too, if you get bored of the natural scenery.

KARON BEACH
หาดกะรน

Karon Beach is big and wide, another popular spot for visitors, but much less built up than Patong. For some it's a perfect balance between amenities and quiet. Karon is one of the largest beaches on the island, and instead of being bordered by trees or a quiet street, there is a fairly main road adjacent and numerous shops across the street. There will still be some loud water sports such as Jet Skis, but the beach is large enough that noisy activities are confined to the southern end. The village behind the beach is attached to Kata Village, so there is plenty to explore on foot.

★ KATA YAI AND KATA NOI BEACHES
หาดกะตะใหญ่และกะตะน้อย

Kata Beach divides itself into Kata Yai Beach and Kata Noi Beach. What's so great about Kata Beach is what it's missing. Most of the land directly in front of Kata Yai, separated by a narrow lane, is used by an enormous but discreet Club Med, virtually

Patong Beach

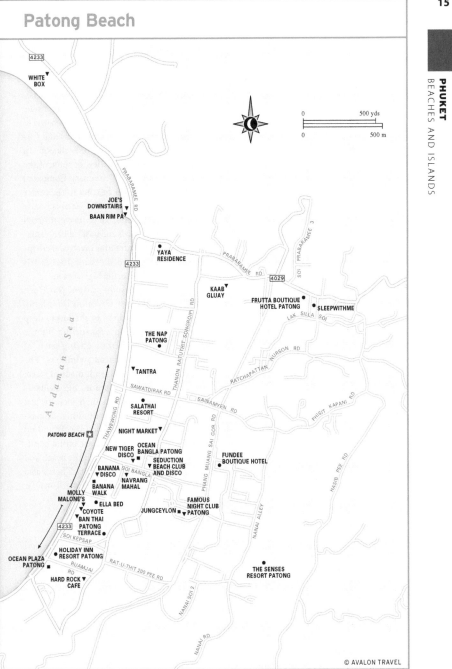

4233

WHITE
BOX

0   500 yds
0   500 m

PRABARAMEE RD

JOE'S
DOWNSTAIRS
BAAN RIM PA

YAYA
RESIDENCE

PRABARAMEE RD

SOI PRABARAMEE 3

4233

4029

KAAB
GLUAY

FRUTTA BOUTIQUE
HOTEL PATONG   SLEEPWITHME

LAK SILLA SOI

THANON RATUTRIT SONGROIPI RD

THE NAP
PATONG

NURSON RD

TANTRA

RATCHAPATTAN RD

SAWATDIRAK RD

SAINAMYEN RD

PHISIT KAPANI RD

THAWEWONG RD

SALATHAI
RESORT

PATONG BEACH ✫

NIGHT MARKET

NEW TIGER
DISCO

OCEAN
BANGLA PATONG

SEDUCTION
BEACH CLUB
AND DISCO

SOI BANGLA

PHANG MUANG SAI GOR RD

FUNDEE
BOUTIQUE HOTEL

HASIB PEE RD

BANANA
DISCO

BANANA
WALK

NAVRANG
MAHAL

MOLLY
MALONE'S

ELLA BED

COYOTE

BAN THAI

4233   PATONG
TERRACE

FAMOUS
NIGHT CLUB
PATONG

JUNGCEYLON

NANAI ALLEY

SOI KEPSAP

HOLIDAY INN
RESORT PATONG

OCEAN PLAZA
PATONG

RUAMJAI
RD

RAT-U-THIT 200 PEE RD

HARD ROCK
CAFE

THE SENSES
RESORT PATONG

NANAI SOI 2

NANAI RD

Andaman Sea

© AVALON TRAVEL

Karon Beach

LE MERIDIEN
PHUKET BEACH RESORT

WISET RD.

PATAK RD.
SOI 24

PHUNAWA RESORT

CENTARA GRAND
BEACH RESORT PHUKET

MANDARAVA
RESORT AND SPA

PATAK
SOI 20

Andaman
Sea

Karon Beach

TWO CHEFS
BAR AND GRILL

KANITA
RESORT &
CAMPING

SIMPLITEL
HOTEL

PATAK
RD.

PATAK RD.

PATAK
SOI 18

0   500 yds
0   500 m

© AVALON TRAVEL

ensuring that there will be no high-rise hotels or other development on the spot for years to come. Kata Yai's beach is used by another high-end hotel (the beach is not private, but some access points are only for hotel guests). As a result, Kata, just south of Karon Beach, is one of the few large beaches on the island without a built-up boardwalk of sorts. That doesn't mean there are no amenities, however. *Som tam*, pad thai, and roti vendors set up stalls in the parking lot every day, there are public showers and restrooms across the lane, and some of the nicest waterfront restaurants on the island are right on the beach. In the low season, the beach attracts surfers looking to take advantage of the waves as well as surf instructors and board-rental stands.

The Kata and Karon area also has some great relaxed nightlife if you're looking for a place to have a drink and listen to live music. Behind the beach area is a small village in the hills, filled with everything you would expect from a beach town—restaurants, cafés, small shops selling local products, and many tailors trying to lure in passing travelers. In fact, Kata Village has developed so much in the past few years that there are also chain restaurants and even fast food. Don't worry, though, it hasn't lost its charm or beach town feeling.

NAI HARN BEACH
หาดในหาน

Nearly at the southern tip of the island is the secluded Nai Harn Beach, with a small coastline set off by long strips of land on either side. The area right behind the beach is a patch of casuarina pine trees, offering shade and further enhancing the feeling of seclusion. In front, there's a beautiful view of some of the rock formations just off the coast. Compared with some of the other beaches in the center of the island's west coast, Nai Harn is a little more difficult to access, but the drive, through winding country roads and past rubber plantations, is worth the extra time involved. Perhaps because it's at the end of the island, the beach is less crowded, even during high season.

During the monsoon season, Nai Harn often has the biggest waves on the island, thanks to a quick drop from shallow to deep water. It's a popular spot for surfing, but the waves can be treacherous during parts of the year for inexperienced swimmers. The area right behind Nai Harn is made of steep, stony cliffs, and there are no big roads or built-up areas in the immediate vicinity, just a couple of resorts and a Buddhist monastery. Although there's no boardwalk and no nightlife to speak of, there are still a handful of small shops right next to the beach and even a couple of little restaurants. There's also a bus that goes directly from Phuket Town for 100 baht.

CAPE PHROMTHEP
แหลมพรหมเทพ

The southernmost point of the island, Cape Phromthep, is a small headland jutting out into the sea like the point of a star. It's not a place to go and swim for the day, rather a place to take in the view. This is a popular place for enjoying the sunset.

Kata Yai Beach

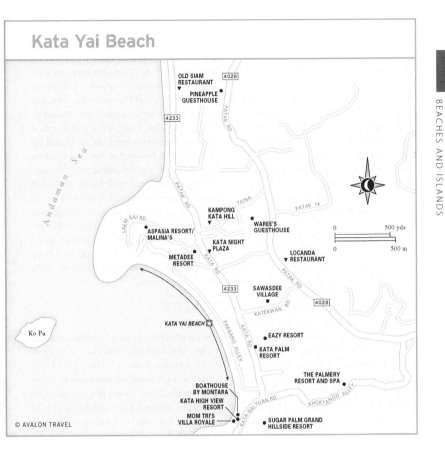

RAWAI BEACH
หาดราไวย์

It's tough to lay out a towel or beach chair and spend the day at Rawai Beach, as many longtail fishing boats are moored here during the day, and the coral fragments on the coast make it really uncomfortable on bare feet for wading in the water. But the area surrounding it is a small fishing village with a wet market selling lots of fresh seafood as well as some touristy souvenirs made from shells, making it a pleasant little excursion if you happen to be in the neighborhood. This is one of the few beaches not facing west, something to keep in mind if you're looking for a sunset view.

CHALONG BAY
อ่าวฉลอง

Chalong Bay is not suitable for swimming, but it serves as the launching point for a number of charter and tour boats heading to different islands off the coast. In the morning the pier is filled with visitors getting ready for excursions, and in the afternoon you'll see the same folks heading back. The little streets surrounding the bay have a relaxed atmosphere and some inexpensive guesthouses, as well as diving and other marine-activity supply shops. In the afternoon and at night, there are a couple of modern restaurants with outdoor seating and great views, perfect if you've just returned from an excursion and are looking for a place to unwind and watch the sunset.

★ KO MAI THON
เกาะไม้ท่อน

Ko Mai Thon is known for some excellent coral formations within snorkeling distance of the shore and can be reached from the mainland in less than an hour. This small island is home to the private Honeymoon Island Resort, so any visits have to be arranged through them. At the time of writing, the resort was under renovation, with no known date of reopening.

KO RACHA
เกาะราชา

Made up of two islands, Racha Yai and Racha Noi, about 13 kilometers (8 mi) off the southern coast of Phuket, Ko Racha is generally visited on diving and snorkeling trips. There are no accommodations on Racha Noi, but now a handful of little bungalows and resorts dot Racha Yai. On Racha Yai the most popular spot to go is Tawan Tok Bay, sometimes called Ao Bungalow. The sand here is very fine and soft. When the seas are calm and the water is clear, this is a great place for snorkeling, especially as it's so close to the mainland.

Racha Noi, which can only be visited on day trips, has some excellent diving at the hard coral reefs off the northern and southern coasts of the island, and it is not uncommon for divers to see manta rays and even occasional whales. There's also a relatively new shipwreck off the southwest coast. Not yet overgrown with sea life, it nonetheless attracts lots of fish and is a fun thing to do if you've never wreck-dived before. Diving off of Racha Noi, however, is not for beginners because of the depths and strong currents. Newbies should stick with Racha Yai, which has some great coral reefs of its own and can easily be viewed by novice divers and even snorkelers. Many dive, snorkel, and touring companies offer day trips to the islands; otherwise, you can get a longtail boat from Chalong Bay if you're interested in going there on your own.

KO LON
เกาะโหลน

Just a few minutes by boat from the mainland is the chilled-out Ko Lon. There's not a ton to do here, but if you're looking for a bit of that desert-island feeling that's easy to get to, it is a good option. There's just one resort on the island, although you can take day trips if you're just interested in hanging out on their sandy beach.

Sights

If you can drag yourself away from the beautiful beaches, Phuket has a number of interesting places to see. Aside from sights geared for visiting tourists, Phuket and the surrounding islands are home to some amazing natural sights, including rainforests, mangrove swamps, karst rock formations rising out of the ocean, and marine areas with colorful fish and coral. Since it is a vacation town, there are tons of fun or silly ways to spend your afternoons, whether taking in a cabaret show or visiting a nature conservation center. They may not be all that culturally significant, but they'll certainly keep you distracted on a rainy day.

INLAND PHUKET
Thalang National Museum
พิพิธภัณฑสถานแห่งชาติถลาง
The Thalang National Museum (Mu 3, Si Sumthon, Thalang, tel. 07/631-1426, 8:30am-4:30pm daily except national holidays, 30B, free under age 7), eponymous with one of Phuket's historical names, houses a number

Phuket Town

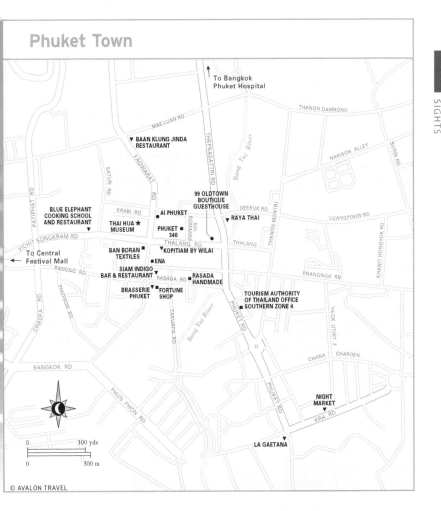

of exhibitions demonstrating Phuket's history and includes some prehistoric artifacts such as stone tools as well as religious items. The museum isn't vast or particularly comprehensive, but there are some entertaining displays reenacting life on the island throughout the ages, including a reenactment of the famous Battle of Thalang, involving the two sister-heroines. The highlight of the museum might be a 9th-century statue of the Hindu god Vishnu, discovered in the forests of Phang Nga about 200 years ago.

Kathu Mining Museum
พิพิธภัณฑ์เหมืองแร่ภูเก็ต

The **Kathu Mining Museum** (Mu 5, Kathu Ko Kaew Rd., Kathu, tel. 08/8766-0962, 9am-4pm daily except national holidays, 100B foreigners, 50B Thais, 50B for foreign children, 20B for Thai children) showcases Phuket's past as a tin mining hub. The museum, in a massive former mansion, has some interesting exhibits that illustrate the daily lives of tin miners and their families, as well as the nuts and bolts, so to speak, of tin mining. Like other museums in Phuket, some of the execution of exhibits seems to miss the mark, and it's not a particularly crowded place, so it can feel a little deserted or aged despite that it's only been open since 2009. Still, since it's relatively close to Patong Beach, it's worth visiting if you're looking for a little information about the island's history.

Khao Phra Thaeo Wildlife Sanctuary
เขตอนุรักษ์พันธุ์ สัตว์ป่าเขาพระแทว

Instead of taking the kids to the zoo, where they'll see animals in captivity, or to monkey, elephant, and crocodile shows bordering on exploitation, bring them to the Khao Phra Thaeo Wildlife Sanctuary (Bang Pae Waterfall, Pa Khao, tel. 02/896-2672, 9am-4pm daily). Covering the only remaining virgin rainforest on the island, the sanctuary is home to barking deer, wild boars, monkeys, lizards, and a host of other creatures as well as some lovely waterfalls such as Namtok Ton Sai and Namtok Bang Pae. The sanctuary is also home to the Gibbon Rehabilitation Project, an organization that takes in formerly captive gibbons and rehabilitates them for return to the wild. Gibbons have been poached to extinction in Phuket but are now kept in captivity on the island, often to lure visitors into bars. The project has been working to reintroduce gibbons to Phuket and has set up a facility at the wildlife sanctuary staffed by volunteers from all over the world who come to feed, care for, and train the animals. The project is open for visitors during the day and also accepts volunteers year-round. There's no admission fee, but they do accept donations.

PHUKET TOWN AND THE EAST COAST
Thai Hua Museum
พิพิธภัณฑ์ภูเก็ตไทยหัว

The Thai Hua Museum (28 Krabi Rd., Muang District, tel. 07/621-1224, 9am-7pm daily except national holidays, 200B foreigners, 50B Thais, free children under 100 cm [40 in] tall) in Phuket Town celebrates the influence of the Chinese who came to Phuket in waves before, during, and after the tin boom. Exhibits focus on everything from business to daily life, and although the museum is small and somewhat limited in scope, it does highlight an important part of the island's history. The museum is one of the nicest and most modern on the island, and it is worth a quick visit if you are in Phuket Town. The

Phuket Aquarium

building the museum is housed in, a classic Sino-Portuguese mansion, is lovely, and there is a pleasant café on the premises should you want to take a break and have a drink.

Phuket Aquarium
สถานแสดงพันธุ์สัตว์น้ำภูเก็ต

The **Phuket Aquarium** (Cape Panwa, 51 Sakdi Det Rd., Phuket Town, tel. 07/639-1126, 9am-5pm daily, 100B adults, 50B children), a part of the Phuket Marine Biological Center, has a collection of ocean and saltwater fish as well as sharks, rays, and sea turtles housed in over 30 tanks. It's a great opportunity to see some of the exotic tropical fish that might have swum by you in the ocean (except for the gigantic cod, which you'll be hoping aren't swimming anywhere near you). The coolest part of the aquarium is a clear tunnel through one of the large tanks, which you can walk through to see the sharks, fish, and rays. For kids, there's a touch pool where they can experience firsthand what a sea cucumber feels like. The center, located at Cape Panwa on the southeast part of the island, also has a

research vessel you can visit when it's not out at sea. Although the aquarium is not quite on par with what you may be used to at home, and it's a far drive if you're not close to Cape Panwa to start, children seem to enjoy it quite a bit.

Phuket Butterfly Farm
สวนผีเสื้อและโลกแมลงภูเก็ต

If you can't get enough of flying insects during your tropical vacation, check out the **Phuket Butterfly Farm** (71/6 Samkong, Phuket Town, tel. 07/621-5616, www.phuketbutterfly.com, 9am-5:30pm daily, 300B adults, 150B under age 10), which is home to tens of thousands of butterflies fluttering around its outdoor garden. There's also an insectarium, with bugs of all types to see, including giant grasshoppers, bugs that look like leaves and sticks, and even tarantulas. The farm is also home to a domesticated otter the staff adopted from its former owner and keeps on the grounds to protect it from the wild. The butterfly farm can arrange to pick you up from your hotel for a small fee.

Entertainment and Events

SHOWS
Fantasea
ภูเก็ตแฟนตาซี

More a Las Vegas spectacle than a mellow evening, **Fantasea** (99 Mu 3, Kamala Beach, tel. 07/638-5000, www.phuket-fantasea.com, 5:30pm-11:30pm Fri.-Wed., dinner 6pm-8:30pm, show begins 9pm, show and dinner 1,200B) can put on a show: Special effects, scores of acrobats and other performers in costume, and even dancing elephants make for quite an event. There's also a buffet dinner, carnival games, and shopping to keep you busy after the program. It's not quite a romantic night out, but it's great for families with children.

NIGHTLIFE
Much of the island's nightlife is centered on Patong Beach, which becomes a sort of red-light district meets frat party come nightfall. There are scores of bars and discos packing in the travelers, and music and people seem to pour out of every doorway into the streets surrounding Bangla Road. The music is almost always pop, Top 40, or techno. If that's not your scene, it can be tough to find live music venues or sophisticated places to hang your hat, get your drink on, or do a little dancing. Although there are plenty of high-end accommodations, this trend historically has not spilled over into the nightlife choices, and many visitors not interested in extreme partying tend to spend their nights hanging out at the bars

in their hotel or resort. That may be changing, as small bars sans working women or eardrum-bursting music are beginning to appear in small numbers.

The nightlife scene in Phuket is very fluid, and bars and clubs that were popular a year ago may already be closed down, or reincarnated with a different name, by the time you visit. Bars generally close at 1am, nightclubs at 2am, although those rules are sometimes less strictly enforced in Phuket.

Patong Beach

New Tiger Disco (Bangla Rd., tel. 07/634-5112, 7pm-2am daily, no cover), which opened in 2013 after the old Tiger Disco burned down in 2012, is one of the most popular places to go at night in Patong. The tiger theme is over the top, with statues of roaring tigers all over the massive three-story complex that literally shakes because the music is so loud at night. There are multiple independent bars in the complex, and though all are welcome at these establishments, with explicit names and lots of scantily clad women, there is definitely a target market.

Seduction Beach Club and Disco (39/1 Bangla Rd., tel. 08/2776-7949, 10pm-late daily, cover 200B) attracts a young crowd of mostly travelers who like to dance and drink. Ibiza-style electronic dance music with a little hip-hop thrown in seems to be the music of choice here, which seems to work well for the crowd it attracts. The ambiance is much less seedy than other bars on this *soi*.

Famous Night Club Patong (Jungceylon Shopping Complex, tel. 07/636-6717, 1pm-late daily, no cover) on the roof of the Jungceylon mall, positions itself as a classy, upscale nightclub and for the most part delivers, though with a crowd of mostly young travelers it's hard to keep the promise entirely. Aside from the swanky interior, the big attraction is the glass-bottom swimming pool: From the dance floor below you can watch people swimming above. And if you feel like taking a swim, know you're being watched, too!

Banana Disco (96 Thawewong Rd., tel.

08/1271-2469, 7pm-2am daily, cover 200B) is one of the area's most popular nightclubs. Despite (or maybe because of) the name, it seems to attract lots of young, single local women. Though it is known as a pickup joint, it doesn't feel too sleazy, especially compared to the choices on Bangla Road. The music selection is techno and pop, and the cover charge includes one drink.

If you're looking for some nightlife that doesn't involve loud music and dressing up, there are some good pubs and bars in Patong, too. Molly Malone's (94/1 Thawewong Rd., tel. 07/629-2771, 10am-late daily, no cover) is your standard Irish bar, which means you'll find decent Western food, beer, and lots of football on television. There is also live music most nights and pool tables.

Hard Rock Cafe (48/1 Ruamjai Rd., tel. 07/636-6381, 11am-2am daily, no cover) has live music, nachos, cheeseburgers, and lots of music memorabilia. It's also quite expensive compared to other live music venues on the island, but if you are looking for a reliable, no-surprises place to go, it might be worth the cost.

FESTIVALS AND EVENTS

Most events are scheduled according to the lunar calendar, so dates change from year to year. Make sure to check with the Tourism Authority of Thailand (tel. 02/250-5500, www.tourismthailand.org) for specific dates when you are visiting.

Chinese New Year

In Phuket, Chinese New Year (Jan. or Feb.) is celebrated with the Phuket Old Town Festival, which celebrates the island's Chinese heritage. The locus of the celebration is in Phuket's Old Town, and the main streets are closed off for three days to make room for song and dance performances. There are also art exhibits and other events around the city. Although everyone in the Old Town will be celebrating, the beach areas will have fewer events.

Songkran

Phuket, and just about every other place in Thailand, goes wild during the traditional new year celebration of Songkran (Apr.). For three full days, locals and visitors pour out into the streets to pour water on each other. The ritual was probably originally intended to symbolically wash away sins and bad luck. Nowadays, in all popular beach areas, people bring out big water guns and buckets of water, so expect to get soaked. If you're visiting during this time, some businesses will be closed.

Phuket Vegetarian Festival

For nine days each year, during the Phuket Vegetarian Festival (Sept.), vegetarian food dominates the city. Special vegetarian fare can be found everywhere, from street stalls to high-end restaurants. Even carnivores will enjoy trying their favorite Thai dishes without meat. You'll be able to find them at any restaurant or stall adorned with yellow flags. The festival, which has roots in Chinese traditions but also some elements of Hinduism, originated in Phuket and later spread to other parts of the country. The island is the place it is most intensely celebrated, and during the festival there are ceremonies at many of Phuket's Chinese temples, plus street processions where participants engage in what can only be described as physical torture. Walking on hot coals and piercing oneself with spears and hooks are common activities among participants, so spectating is definitely not for the fainthearted or children.

Loi Krathong

One of Thailand's most beautiful celebrations,

Loi Krathong (Oct.-Nov.) takes place each year on the evening of the 12th full moon of the Thai lunar year (usually October or November). At all major beaches in Phuket, thousands of people launch small floats covered in flowers and candles. The floats, or *krathong,* symbolize the letting go of bad luck and bad feelings, and the holiday is usually celebrated by couples. Don't worry if you didn't bring your own float; there will be plenty of vendors selling them.

Laguna Phuket Triathlon

The popular Laguna Phuket Triathlon (Nov.) attracts people from all over the region. Set in the Laguna Phuket complex of resorts, it has triathletes swimming through a lagoon, into the Andaman Sea, then biking the hills of Phuket and finishing with a flat run around the large Laguna complex. The distances, a 1.8-kilometer (1 mi) swim, 55-kilometer (34 mi) bike ride, and 12 km (7.5 mi) run, are not regulation, but they are a bit longer than an Olympic triathlon. The event has been going on for two decades and is very popular, so sign up well in advance if you are considering competing.

King's Cup Regatta

Billed as Asia's biggest and most popular regatta, the King's Cup Regatta (Dec.) takes place over the course of a week in December. It has been going on since 1987 and continues to grow in size and popularity. Even if you're not competing, you can enjoy watching and try to crash (or snag an invite to) one of the many parties surrounding the event.

Shopping

If you're just looking for small souvenirs to take home, every village near every beach has small items such as seashells or Thai-styled handicrafts. There are some small shops throughout the island selling items that are

a little more authentic, as well as some high-end antiques stores, some gem stores, and even full-fledged shopping malls.

If you're shopping for gems or antiques on the island, it's difficult to ensure you are getting a good deal unless you have some amount of expertise to evaluate the merchandise. Although there are some good deals to be had, there is no redress should you get home and realize you are unhappy with your purchase.

There are a couple of large shopping malls on the island, serving both visitors and the year-round folks—a real convenience if you find you've forgotten something from home.

PATONG AND VICINITY

Patong's shopping scene has gotten increasingly sophisticated and increasingly convenient. Aside from the massive Jungceylon shopping mall, the main beach road has more and more places to spend money every year.

Jungceylon (181 Rat-U-Thit 200 Pee Rd., Patong, tel. 07/660-0111, 11am-midnight daily) is about a 10-minute walk from Patong Beach up Soi Bangla. The mall, which opened in 2007, is a considerable step up from the shopping that was previously available in the area. There's a full-sized Robinson Department Store, a Carrefour hypermarket stocked with food, appliances, electronics, and everything in between, and many other stores to fulfill your shopping needs. The mall also has a nice little food court in the basement, serving up noodle and rice dishes, smoothies, and even fresh seafood. Aside from the food court, the bottom level also houses That's Siam. This shop, really a group of small shops, carries scores of Thai handicrafts and other decorative items, including home textiles, silk products, and delicious-smelling bath and body goodies.

Banana Walk (124/11 Taweewong Rd., Patong, tel. 08/1987-1148, 10am-10pm daily), right on the main beach road in Patong, is a small, upscale shopping mall with some clothing stores, gift shops, a couple of electronics stores, and plenty of restaurants. There is also a Boots drugstore and a small Villa supermarket on the premises. Hours of individual shops may vary.

The Ocean Group has two midsize shopping malls in Patong, Ocean Plaza Patong (48 Taweewong Rd., Patong, tel. 07/634-1297, 10am-10pm daily) and Ocean Bangla Patong (31 Bangla Rd., Patong, tel. 07/634-1163, 10am-10pm daily). These midmarket malls are a little hectic and less modern than the newest shopping malls in the area, but in addition to all the stand-alone stores, both have lots of market carts and stalls selling souvenirs, clothes, and shoes, plus good food courts with mostly Thai dishes.

Jungceylon shopping mall

NORTHERN WEST COAST

This area is where you'll find lots of antiques shops and galleries, catering mainly to people who are furnishing villas they've purchased on the island.

Oriental Fine Art (106/19-20 Bangtao Rd., Thalang, tel. 07/632-5141, 9am-8pm daily) is a large multistory shop that feels more like a gallery for Asian sculpture, except that you can buy everything on display. They also carry furniture, mainly with classic Chinese styling, and will arrange worldwide shipping.

Songtique (8/48-49 Srisoontorn Rd., Cherngtalay, tel. 08/1668-2555, 9am-6pm Mon.-Sat.) carries mostly original-period Buddha images and reproductions. Some of the pieces are stunningly larger than life, although the owner also stocks images small enough to take home with you. There is also a selection of antique Chinese furniture. This store is worth dropping by just to see the beautiful Buddhas.

On the road to Laguna Phuket, there are a handful of furniture and antiques stores. Heritage Collection (60 Phuket Laguna Rd., tel. 07/632-5818, 9am-8pm daily) has an inventory of beautiful antiques from China and Southeast Asia. There are Chinese chests,

paintings, sculptures, and plenty of Buddhist objects in this large shop.

For more contemporary items, Ceramics of Phuket (185/6 Mu 7, Srisoontorn Rd., Thalang, tel. 07/627-2151, 8am-5pm Mon.-Sat.) carries vases, display bowls, and decorative figures, all from a local designer.

Located in the swanky Plaza Surin, Ginger Shop (Plaza Surin, 5/50 Mu 3, Cherngtalay, Thalang, tel. 07/627-1616, 10am-8pm daily) is a fun shop carrying everything from cushions to glassware and even spa products. What really sets the shop apart, though, is the clothing and women's accessories. There's a lot of beading going on in their collection of tops, dresses, bags, and scarves, but since they design their clothes with contemporary lines, the result looks modern and just a little funky.

PHUKET TOWN

Just outside of the center of Phuket Town is the large, convenient Central Festival Mall (74/75 Mu 5, 5 Vichitsongkram Rd., tel. 07/629-1111, 10:30am-11pm daily), which has a large high-end department store, a sports store, a bookstore, and plenty of other shops carrying both local and international products. The mall also has a large movie theater, multiple restaurants, and a food court. In

Phuket Town's fashionable shopping scene

2014, it underwent a major renovation to upgrade the facilities.

Ban Boran Textiles (51 Yaworat Rd., tel. 07/621-1563, 10:30am-6:30pm Mon.-Sat.), a funky little shop in Phuket Town, sells a nice selection of mostly handwoven textiles from Thailand and other countries in the region. Offerings include wall hangings as well as clothing, and prices are quite reasonable. There are also some curios and decorative jewelry.

ENA (52 Yaworat Rd., tel. 08/9651-9973, 10:30am-6:30pm Mon.-Sat.) is a lovely little textiles shop that specializes in clothing, scarves, handbags, and home decor made from fabrics produced in the region. Prices are reasonable, and this shop usually has a good stock of inventory despite its small size.

Rasada Handmade (29 Rasada Rd., tel. 07/635-5439, 9:30am-7pm Mon.-Sat.) is another little shop specializing in textiles and small objects for the home that stocks items such as bedcovers, tablecloths, and Buddhist figures.

For more upscale decorator objects, stop in at Fine Orient (51/20 Chaofa West Rd., tel. 07/652-1552, 10:30am-5:30pm Thurs.-Tues.). The shop specializes in reproduction and antique furniture from China but also carries furniture and other items from neighboring countries. Many of the things sold here are beautiful, expensive, and too big to fit in a suitcase. The shop will arrange shipping for anything you buy there.

Kai Tak Interior Designs (Royal Phuket Marina, 63/202 Thep Kasattri Rd., tel. 07/636-0891, 9am-7pm Mon.-Sat.) carries some beautiful furniture and decorator items from all over the region. The prices here are on the high to very high end, but the shop is worth visiting if only to look at what they've got.

Fortune Shop (12-16 Rasada Rd., tel. 07/621-6238, 9:30am-7pm Mon.-Sat., 10am-3pm Sun.) has lots of small Thai souvenir items, including Thai silk decorative pillows and wall hangings, pottery, jewelry, and spa products. This is a great one-stop shop if you're looking to pick up some nice gifts to bring home.

Sports and Recreation

DIVING

The waters surrounding Phuket offer an amazing diversity of marinelife and dive sites from beginner to advanced. Some of these sites are considered among the best in the world. Hundreds of dive shops offer courses, equipment rental, day trips, and live-aboards (where you live aboard a boat for a few days). If you're planning on diving in the region, don't worry too much about where you are staying relative to the areas where you want to dive; most diving shops offer dives to all of the most popular sites in the region.

The area surrounding the main island offers some good diving day trips. Ko Racha Noi is a popular place to visit on a day trip and has a nice mix of both colorful coral and challenging, rocky terrain. Another very popular destination is Shark Point, about 32 kilometers (20 mi) east of Chalong Bay. There are three rock outcroppings that attract—as the name implies—sharks (mostly leopard sharks). Just under one kilometer (0.6 mi) away is Anemone Reef, with lots of anemone, coral, and plenty of colorful small fish. If you're interested in wreck diving, close by is King Cruiser Wreck, a sunken car ferry in Phang Nga Bay. This site is appropriate for most divers and attracts lots of fish. Other wrecks near Phuket, including SS Petaling, HMS Squirrel, and HMS Vestal, are considered technical dives and can only be visited by experienced divers.

Certification

In Thailand most diving instruction courses offer PADI (www.padi.com) open-water diver certification. These courses take 3-4 days, at the end of which you'll be certified to dive all over the world. You'll spend time in the classroom first learning about safety and dive theory, take your first dive in a swimming pool, and advance to supervised open-water dives. Expect to pay 10,000-15,000 baht for the full course, including equipment and dives. If you can't imagine wasting hours inside a classroom while you're on vacation, and assuming there is a PADI training center where you live, you can do the classroom and pool-diving components of your training at home and bring your referral paperwork with you to Thailand, where you'll be able to complete the open-water portion of the certification.

Certified divers looking to advance their skills can also take dive master courses, become certified diving instructors, and arrange training internships at some of the larger training centers. These programs are at least two weeks long and cost 30,000-75,000 baht.

Recompression Chambers

Although accidents and the bends are quite rare, Badalveda Diving Medical Center at Bangkok Hospital Phuket (2/1 Thanon Hongyok Utis, Phuket Town, tel. 07/625-4425, 24-hour emergency hotline tel. 08/1989-9482) has a hyperbaric chamber and medical staff who specialize in diving injuries.

Dive Shops and Centers

When choosing a company to go diving with, first check the PADI website, which lists all of the PADI-certified dive shops across the globe and is searchable by country. There are many excellent dive shops and training centers throughout the Andaman region, and Thailand in general has an excellent safety record when it comes to diving. Instructors and dive masters are both local and foreign, and all are fluent in English. To pick a dive shop, it's best to drop in to some in your vicinity and spend a few minutes talking to staff before deciding who to dive or train with. The following dive centers are all certified by PADI to offer open-water diving certification, dive master training, and instructor training. All also offer one-day trips and multiday live-aboard diving trips.

- Dive Asia (24 Thanon Karon, Kata Beach, tel. 07/633-0598, www.diveasia.com)
- Kata Diving Service (Kata Garden Resort, 121/1 Mu 4, Thanon Patak, Karon Beach, tel. 07/633-0392)
- Marina Divers (45 Thanon Karon, Karon Beach, tel. 07/633-0272)
- Oceanic Divecenter (30 Thanon Karon, Karon Beach, tel. 07/633-3043, www.oceanicdivecenter.com)
- Pro-Tech Dive College (389 Thanon Patak, Karon Beach, tel. 07/628-6112, www.protechdivers.com)
- Sea Dragon Dive Center (5/51 Mu 7, Thanon Khuek Khak, Khao Lak, Phang Nga, tel. 07/648-5420, www.seadragondivecenter.com)
- Sea Fun Divers (Katathani Beach Resort, 14 Kata Noi Rd., Kata Noi Beach, tel. 07/633-0124, www.seafundivers.com)
- Sea World Dive Team (177/23 Soi Sansabai, Patong Beach, tel. 07/634-1595, www.seaworld-phuket.com)
- Sunrise Diving (49 Thanon Thawewong, Patong Beach, tel. 07/629-2052)
- Visa Diving (77 Mu 7, Ko Phi Phi, tel. 07/560-1157, www.visadiving.com)
- Warm Water Divers (229 Thanon Rat-U-Thit 200 Pee Rd., Patong Beach, tel. 07/629-2201, www.warmwaterdivers.com)
- West Coast Divers (120/1-3 Rat-U-Thit 200 Pee Rd., Patong Beach, tel. 07/634-1673, www.westcoastdivers.com)

SNORKELING

If you're not a diver, there is still a lot to see in relatively shallow waters if you're armed with a snorkel and a mask. The north end of Patong Beach, the north end of Kata Beach, the south end of Karon Beach, and the north end of Kamala Beach have lovely coral or rocks just off the coast, and you'll definitely see some tropical fish around most of the beaches even if the bottom of the sea is sandy. Otherwise, you can arrange a day trip to tour some of the islands

Drowning Hazards

During high season, the Andaman Sea is often calm and clear, with few waves and no dangerous tides. But during the April-October monsoon season in the low season, the sea can become deadly, especially if there is a storm in the surrounding area. Dozens of people drown in Phuket every year, both locals and visitors.

Phuket has a flag system on all of its beaches, and anytime you see a red flag, it means authorities have decided that the waves and undercurrent are too dangerous. Swimming is not advised at these times, although during low season there are generally no lifeguards around to enforce this rule on even the most popular beaches.

For surfers, this is the best time of year to be in Phuket, as the waves are great, particularly on Nai Harn and Kata Beaches. It's also a great time to learn how to surf, as you can rent a board for a few hundred baht at Kata and even take some lessons at one of the many casual surf schools that set up shop on the south end of the beach. But if you are not a strong swimmer, stay out of the water or remain very close to shore.

---

in Phang Nga Bay, which will include some snorkeling time. Most tour providers will rent snorkels and fins, too. These tours are almost exclusively sold through travel agents, and there are scores of them in Phuket. Some outfitters offering tours are Oceanic Divecenter (30 Thanon Karon, Karon Beach, Phuket, tel. 07/633-3043, www.oceanicdivecenter.com), Sea World Dive Team (177/23 Soi Sansabai, Patong Beach, tel. 07/634-1595, www.seaworld-phuket.com), and Warm Water Divers (229 Thanon Rat-U-Thit 200 Pee, Patong Beach, Phuket, tel. 07/629-2201, www.warmwaterdivers.com). If you're buying a snorkeling trip, make sure to ask how much time you'll spend on the boat versus in the water, the type of boat you'll travel on, and the islands you'll visit.

SEA KAYAKING

Most of the sea kayaking and sea canoeing trips that originate in Phuket will involve taking a motorboat to Phang Nga Bay, where you'll explore the smaller islands, lagoons, and caves for the day before being shuttled back to the big island. Paddling around Phang Nga Bay is a spectacular way to see the area. You can get up close to many of the smaller islands with no beaches to land on, and as opposed to a speedboat tour, you'll

be traveling slowly enough to look closely at the nature around you. Most guides will require only that you are in reasonably good shape to participate. Some will also even paddle for you, should you wish to just sit back and enjoy the scenery. If you're already an experienced paddler, these group tours may feel a little slow, but all of the tour guides can arrange personalized itineraries if you give them enough notice. Sea Canoe (367/4 Yaowarat Rd., Phuket Town, tel. 07/621-2172, www.seacanoe.net) has trips that run from one day to one week and has been running trips in the Andaman every day for nearly 20 years.

Andaman Sea Kayak (tel. 07/623-5353, www.andamanseakayak.com) also has one-day and multiday trips from Phuket, which they combine with camping in a national park. Day trips start around 3,200 baht per person.

Experienced paddlers may want to rent their own kayaks to explore the islands. Paddle Asia (tel. 07/624-0952, www.paddleasia.com) rents well-maintained, high-quality kayaks, although they will only rent to experienced kayakers. If you are not experienced or familiar with the area, unguided kayaking is not recommended unless you're paddling around close to the shore. Many area beaches are filled with Jet Skis and speedboats, and fishing boats travel frequently between beaches and islands.

PADDLE BOARDING

Paddle boarding, or stand-up paddling, has become a very popular sport in Phuket over the past few years. The high season, when there are very few waves, is the best time of year to do it. During rainy season the sea is too choppy (though it's a good time to surf if you're looking for an alternative board sport). There are paddle board schools and rental shops opening all over the island, though some will only be open during high season.

Stand Up Paddle Thailand (131/34 Mu 4, Thalang, Phuket, tel. 07/662-0201, www.standuppaddlethai.com), close to Layan Beach, rents and sells equipment and can suggest places in the area to take lessons. Starboard Stand Up Paddle Board (at Phuket Windsurfing Shop, 37/10 Mu 1, Rawai, Phuket, tel. 087/888-8244, www.isup.asia/index.php/paddle-phuket) rents and sells equipment, does repairs, and offers individual and group lessons. They will deliver equipment to you.

If you are in the Karon Beach area, visit SSS Phuket (122/1 Patak Rd., Karon Beach, Phuket, tel. 07/628-4070, www.sssphuket.com) for rentals and lessons. For lessons, rentals, and tours, plus cocktails, Thai food, and a cool place to hang out on Kamala Beach, visit Skyla's Surf and SUP Club (Kamala Beach, North End, Phuket, tel. 082/519-3282, www.skylaphuket.com).

SAILING AND SPEEDBOAT CHARTERS

There are a number of sailing companies that offer everything from just the sailboat to a whole crew. If you have the time and money, spending a week sailing around the Andaman coast is a luxury adventure you'll never forget. For large groups, the cost of chartering a sailboat and doing some private island-hopping can be even cheaper than staying on a resort, and all the charter companies will take care of food, supplies, and fuel. Chartering a sailboat or speedboat will cost 15,000-100,000 baht per day, depending on the type of vessel and whether it has a crew.

Phuket Sailing (20/28 Soi Suksan 2, Mu 4, Tambon Rawai, Amphoe Muang, tel. 07/628-9656 or 08/1895-1826, www.phuket-sailing.com) offers both crewed and non-crewed boats and will help you design an itinerary. Yacht Pro (adjacent to Yacht Haven

Speed boat tours from Phuket are popular.

Marina, tel. 07/634-8117 to 07/634-8119, www.sailing-thailand.com) has day sailing trips and also offers lessons.

If you're interested in sailing in the area around Phuket and you have your own boat, there are three separate marinas, the Phuket Boat Lagoon, Royal Phuket Marina, and Yacht Haven Phuket Marina, with year-round anchorage.

GOLF

Phuket boasts a handful of well-maintained golf courses open to visitors. Playing on courses surrounded by palm trees and over-looking the ocean is a real treat. Although you can walk on during the low season, it is essential to make reservations as far in advance as possible during the high season, when the cooler weather makes a day on the greens that much more enjoyable. Caddies are obligatory at all of the clubs.

Located closer to the east coast near Phuket Town, the Phuket Country Club (80/1 Mu 7, Vichitsongkram Rd., Kathu, tel. 07/631-9200, www.phuketcountryclub.com, 3,000B) has an 18-hole par-72 course over a former tin mine. The course is great for less-experienced players, although it's not as challenging for low-handicappers.

Set between Phuket Town and Patong Beach in the middle of the island, the Loch Palm Golf Club (38 Mu 5, Vichitsongkram Rd., Kathu, tel. 07/632-1929, www.lochpalm.com, 3,000B) is a hilly course but otherwise good for beginner golfers.

One of the island's newest courses, Red Mountain Golf Course (38 Mu 5, Vichitsongkram Rd., Kathu, tel. 07/632-1929, 4,500B), in the middle of the island, opened in 2007 on another former tin mine. This course is well designed for shorter hitters, and there are lots of slopes and water to contend with.

Located at the Laguna Phuket, home to a handful of luxury resorts, the Laguna Phuket Golf Club (34 Mu 4, Srisoonthorn Rd., Cherngtalay, tel. 07/627-0991, www.lagunaphuket.com/golfclub, 3,400B) has an

18-hole par-71 course with great views of the Andaman Sea.

Although Thai Muang Golf (157/12 Mu 9, Limdul Rd., Thai Muang, Phang Nga, tel. 07/657-1533, www.thaimuanggolfcourse.com, 2,200B) isn't the fanciest course in the area, it does have the only course set right next to the beach. But for the view, you'll have to travel a bit, as the course is actually about an hour's drive off the island in Phang Nga.

Blue Canyon (165 Mu 1, Thep Kasattri Rd., Thalang, tel. 07/632-8088, www.bluecanyonclub.com, canyon course 5,600B, lakes course 4,000B) has two separate 18-hole courses. The lakes course, as the name implies, is surrounded by small water hazards on 17 of the 18 holes. The canyon course, home to the Johnnie Walker Classic, is the nicest in Phuket and has been played by the likes of Tiger Woods and Ernie Els.

The Nicklaus Design Mission Hills Phuket Golf Club (195 Mu 4, Pla Khlock, Thalang, tel. 07/631-0888, www.missionhillsphuket.com, 3,800B) has both an 18-hole and a separate 9-hole course and is located in the northeast part of the island. This is a favorite course among regular golfers on the island, with not only great views of the ocean but also challenging sea breezes to contend with.

GO-KARTS

If you get really bored staring at the beautiful views or island-hopping and want to try something a little more adventurous on land, check out the Patong Go Kart Speedway (118/5 Vichitsongkram Rd., Mu 7, Kathu, tel. 07/632-1949, 10am-7pm daily Nov.-May, from 1,000B). You can spend your time circling the course or practice a few times before you compete in a Grand Prix race with other participants. Kids have to be at least age 16 unless they're participating in one of the kids-only races. Make sure to book ahead, as the course is very popular.

CYCLING

If you're interested in touring the island on two wheels, Action Holidays Phuket (10/195 Jomthong Thani 5/4 Kwang Rd., Phuket Town, tel. 07/626-3575, www.biketoursthailand.com) offers full-day (2,400B) and half-day (1,400B) bike tours around the island. Most of the tours will keep you in the less-touristed eastern part of the island and are a great way to see some smaller villages and rubber plantations. They also offer tours of a neighboring island, Ko Yao Noi, that start in Phuket and involve a short boat ride.

Accommodations

Phuket already has over a thousand accommodations options along the coast, and new ones are being built every year. While it may be hard to find that secluded beach ambiance when all you can see around you are hotels, guesthouses, and cranes building them, the competition keeps costs very competitive, especially during the low season. If you're willing to pay for it, there are still quiet places on the island, and some of the high-end resorts even have small private or semiprivate beaches. And if you stay in the northern part of the island, around the airport, you'll find the beaches much less crowded. If you're traveling with children, bear in mind that Patong Beach can get pretty seedy at night. There are plenty of discos and clubs catering to both gay and straight clientele, and passing through the nightlife neighborhood at night is difficult to avoid if you're staying here.

While you'll still be able to find a few inexpensive bungalows on the beaches in the northern part of the island, if you're basing yourself in the southern part of Phuket or anywhere around Patong Beach, inexpensive accommodations are almost exclusively guesthouses set inland from the beach, and you'll need to walk at least a few minutes to get to the water. In those areas, waterfront rooms are only available at midrange and high-end resorts.

MAI KHAO BEACH
Under 1,500B

With all of the development going on, it's surprising that cheap, simple beach bungalows such as Mai Khao Beach Seaside Cottages (Mai Khao Beach, tel. 08/1895-1233, www. mai-khao-beach.com, 600B) still exist. The very basic thatched-roof huts have mattresses on the floor, no air-conditioning—only fans— and have shared bathrooms with cold-water showers. Mai Khao Beach is a very quiet spot with limited amenities, but there is a beachfront restaurant on the premises serving good inexpensive Thai food. There are also nicer, fan-cooled beachside cottages with en-suite bathrooms if you want to spend a little more. There is a two-night minimum at this property.

Though it's not on the beach (it's about a mile inland), Phuket Camp Ground (137/7 Mu 3, Baan Dan Yit, Mai Khao Beach, tel. 08/1370-1579, www.phuketcampground. com, 500B) is set on a lake and offers a very pretty location to either pitch a tent or rent one of the property's tents. There are also air-conditioned bungalows available for those who like the surroundings but prefer not to camp. There is a restaurant and canteen on the premises.

The bungalows at Bungalow@Maikhao (128 Mu 3, Mai Khao Beach, tel. 08/3391-3960, 1,200B) aren't fancy but do offer en-suite bathrooms and air-conditioning, a step above the typical beach bungalow experience. Mai Khao in general is not very crowded, but because there is not too much development around this property in particular, it can feel very remote. The on-site restaurant serves Thai food and drinks, but closes early. Take the long walk to the neighboring Holiday Inn if you want something late at night.

1,500-3,000B

Near Bungalow@Maikhao, but almost twice the price, is the large Holiday Inn Phuket Mai Khao Beach Resort (81 Mu 3, Mai

Khao Beach, tel. 07/660-3699, www.ihg. com, 2,800B), which offers guests comfortable, modern rooms, a massive swimming pool that spreads out from one end of the resort to the other, and plenty of other facilities, including a kids' club. Though the resort is popular among couples and groups of adults, it is very family-friendly and there are family suites with rooms designed specially for young children. The resort is right on the beach, and there is a small sunbathing area set up with chairs and towels for guests. There are limited places to eat within walking distance, but plenty of hotel restaurants and bars.

Over 4,500B

Repeat visitors to Phuket often say the JW Marriott (231 Mu 3, Mai Khao Beach, tel. 07/633-8000, www.marriott.com, 4,500B) is their favorite hotel on the island, perhaps because of the top-notch facilities and quiet, scenic location on Mai Khao Beach. The upscale resort has numerous swimming pools, including a children's pool and a pool with waterslide, a tennis court, a full-service spa, plus plenty of planned activities every week, including bicycle tours and sailing lessons. The kids' club, and suites and villas with plenty of space for little ones, make this a great choice for families.

The Anantara Phuket Villas (888 Mu 3, Mai Khao Beach, tel. 07/633-6100, www.phuket.anantara.com, 15,000B), on the relatively quiet and peaceful Mai Khao Beach, has luxurious large villas with private pools. The lush property is unmistakably Thai; all the villas are filled with traditional Thai furnishings but are still modern and stylish. The Anantara spa is likewise luxurious and traditional, and though treatments can be pricey, the surroundings make it worth the cost. Service is discreet, but staffers are very focused on making sure guests are well taken care of. For an indulgent, romantic vacation in a secluded spot on a beautiful beach, the Anantara will not disappoint.

NAI YANG BEACH
Under 1,500B

If you can manage to snag one of the six bungalows at Tanamas House (57/16 Mu 1, Nai Yang Beach, tel. 07/620-5218, www.tanamas-house.com, 1,200B), within walking distance of Nai Yang Beach, consider yourself lucky. Tanamas House is a true value property and a great choice for those who want some resort amenities but don't want to pay hundreds of dollars per night for them. The lovely bed-and-breakfast has lush landscaping and a nice swimming pool, and the rooms are small but very clean and comfortable. There is a restaurant on the grounds; if you are looking for something fancier, you can walk to the Indigo Pearl, which has more upscale food and drink options.

Seapines Villa Liberg (111 Mu 5, Soi Bang Malao 2, Nai Yang Beach, tel. 08/1814-4883, www.villalibergphuket.com, 1,200B) offers pretty Thai-style rooms set around a pleasant swimming pool, which is surrounded by a lush, green garden. Rooms have basic decorations and furnishings but are tasteful, clean, and large for the price. Facilities are limited to the swimming pool and a small café that serves a very limited breakfast. On the plus side, the beach is just a hundred meters away.

Panpen Bungalows (65/11 Mu 5, Nai Yang Beach, tel. 08/7469-4797, www.panpenbungalowphuket.com, 1,000B) is very close to Nai Yang Beach and has clean, modern cottages with air-conditioning and private bathrooms. Though it might lack the rustic charm of thatched-roof bungalows, it's definitely going to be cleaner and more comfortable. The property is close to the airport and offers free transfers to and from between 6am and midnight. Many visitors choose to stay here before an early flight out, and the cost of a night's stay in one of the bungalows is just a little more than the cost of an airport transfer from another part of the island.

Chez Charly Bungalow (65/6 Mu 1, Tambon Sakoo, Nai Yang Beach, tel. 07/620-5124, 1,000B) is a small, homey, family-run operation with just a handful of bungalows and studios for rent. Rooms won't win any design awards, but they are far better fitted, and more comfortable, than anything else you'll find in this price range. Plus, the couple who run it are friendly and helpful. It's a 15-minute walk to the beach from here, and food and drink options in the surrounding area are very limited.

1,500-3,000B

Near a quiet, pretty beach is the comfy Golddigger's Resort (74/12 Surin Rd., Nai Yang Beach, tel. 07/632-8424, www.golddigger-resort.com, 2,100B). This very small resort has clean, basically furnished guest rooms and some larger family accommodations that can sleep four people. There's also a nice swimming pool on the grounds, but if you want to go to the beach, it's only a five-minute walk. The decor leaves a lot to be desired, but this is an excellent deal in the off-season, when rates are just over half price.

3,000-4,500B

Dewa Phuket Resort (65 Mu 1, Tambon Sakoo, Nai Yang Beach, tel. 07/637-2300, www.dewaphuketresort.com, 4,000B) has pool villas, suites, and apartments with kitchens and multiple bedrooms for those traveling in larger groups or with children. The pretty, modern Thai-style resort has a massive swimming pool and plenty of activities, such as yoga, to keep guests busy. Like other properties on Nai Yang, Dewa Phuket Resort is not right on the beach; rather, you have to cross a road and walk about five minutes. Though the property bills itself as a boutique property, with nearly 100 rooms it's a bit too large to truly qualify.

Over 4,500B

The Bill Bensley-designed Indigo Pearl (Nai Yang Beach, tel. 07/632-7006, www.indigo-pearl.com, 5,500B) is a standout in the luxury-resort category. Designed to convey Phuket's mining history, the property has cement flooring, exposed beams, and thatched roofs juxtaposed against colorful, modern design elements in addition to verdant landscaping throughout. The guest rooms are as funky as the common space. Expect modern modular furniture and color combinations not often seen in generic hotel rooms. There are also tennis courts, a library, and activities for children. The only drawback is that the resort is not right on the beach; it's a five-minute walk.

NAI THON BEACH

Perhaps the most beautiful and luxurious resort on the island is Trisara (60/1 Mu 6, Srisoonthorn Rd., Nai Thon Beach, tel. 07/631-0100, www.trisara.com, 22,500B). The guest rooms are larger than most city apartments and furnished with impressive teakwood pieces. The multibedroom villas are pricey but come with their own waitstaff, private pools, and amazing views of the ocean. There is also a larger pool at the resort right on the edge of the coast, and a very small private beach for guests.

Nai Thon Mansion (424 Mu 4, Nai Thon Beach, tel. 08/1894-5344, www.naithonbeach-hotelphuket.com, 800B) hits above its weight when it comes to value for money. The rooms at this budget guesthouse are clean, modern, and comfortable, and it's just a few minutes on foot to the beach. If a stand-alone, four-story building is too far off from the thatched-roof beach bungalow you've been imagining, though, you might want to consider another option. However, it is one of the only inexpensive places to stay on tiny Nai Thon.

BANG TAO BEACH AND LAGUNA

Laguna Phuket (390/1 Mu 1, Srisoonthorn Rd., tel. 07/636-2300, www.lagunaphuket.com, 4,000B) is an expansive compound with six separate resorts set around a small lagoon just off the coast. With about 240 hectares of shared space along with private beaches, the resort feels like a large village of its own instead of part of the rest of the island. The land it sits on, now prime property on Bang

Tao Bay, was once a tin mine that had been abandoned, the land left fallow for years. In the 1980s the land was reclaimed at a cost of US$200 million. There's also an 18-hole golf course, tennis courts, activities for children, and even a wedding chapel, should you choose to tie the knot on a romantic vacation. The upside of Laguna Phuket is that it's completely enclosed and has everything you'll need for a relaxing vacation. But that can be a downside, too, as there's little chance to experience Thailand when you're there unless you venture off the compound.

The swankiest, and most expensive, of the resorts is Banyan Tree Laguna (33, 33/27 Mu 4, Srisoonthorn Rd., Nai Yang Beach, tel. 07/632-4374, www.banyantree.com, 14,000B), filled with large luxury villas with small private pools and beautifully manicured grounds. Individual Thai-style villas are decorated with modern furnishings and have separate sitting and sleeping areas. The villas are exceptionally well maintained and feel more like five-star hotel rooms than beach bungalows.

The Allamanda Laguna Phuket (29 Mu 4, Srisoonthorn Rd., tel. 07/632-4359, www.allamandaphuket.com, 3,000B) is a more down-to-earth property and has very spacious suites that are perfect for families or larger groups traveling together. There are three large pools on the property and three separate pools for children; it's hard to get bored hanging out on the property. Although the Allamanda is not directly on the beach, it offers a shuttle to its own beach area with sun chairs and changing rooms.

Outside of the Laguna complex is the Sunwing Resort and Spa (22 Mu 2, Chern Thalay, tel. 07/631-4263, www.sunwingphuket.com, 3,000B), a large, self-contained resort with nearly 300 rooms and suites right on a quiet stretch of beach south of Laguna. The four-star property has clean, modern facilities, a spa, and multiple bars and restaurants. This is a very family-friendly property, with an extensive kids' club and activities for children, rooms and suites designed for families, and multiple swimming pools. It tends to be popular with Scandinavian tourists but attracts guests from all over the world.

SURIN BEACH
Under 1,500B

Surin doesn't have too many budget options, but the Surin Bay Inn (106/11 Mu 3, Surin Beach, tel. 07/627-1601, www.surinbayinn.com, 1,000B) is a good choice if you want clean, basic accommodations a bit nicer than a backpacker guesthouse. All rooms have modern fittings, and bathrooms are more than decent by any standard. Decor is inoffensive, which is an achievement in this price category. The inn is just a few minutes from Surin Beach, across the main road.

1,500-3,000B

The Surintra Resort (106/11 Mu 3, Surin Beach, tel. 07/627-1601, www.surinbayinn.com, 1,500B) is a small property with just enough facilities to call itself a resort, though because the common spaces are very limited and the swimming pool quite small, it would be better called a "micro-resort." Still, for the price and location, just a few minutes on foot to Surin Beach, you can't really expect much more. Rooms are stylish and modern, though there isn't a particular design theme that permeates the whole property.

3,000-4,500B

Right next door to the Twin Palms is the Manathai (121 Srisoonthorn Rd., Surin Beach, tel. 07/627-0900, www.manathai.com, 4,000B). Not quite as swanky or expansive, the Manathai still has pleasant, well-designed, modern guest rooms and excellent, friendly service. Neither of the two pools is large, but they are beautifully laid out with indigo-blue tiles. The common lobby and bar area, which has soaring ceilings and plenty of plush and comfortable sitting areas, almost makes up for the fact that the pools and other common areas are just too small for the number of guest rooms.

In the hills above Surin is Ayara Hilltops (125 Mu 3, Surin Beach, tel. 07/627-1271, www.ayarahilltops.com, 4,000B), an adults-only resort with large, nicely designed Thai-style suites and villas overlooking Surin Bay. The lush, green landscaping and beautiful swimming pool make the resort feel much farther away from the rest of the world than it is, as it's just a five-minute walk down to Surin Beach. Some of the more expensive suites have their own whirlpools or plunge pools. No one under 18 is allowed on the property, and it's a very popular destination for couples on romantic holidays.

Over 4,500B

Situated in Surin, just across the main road from the beach, ★ Twin Palms (106/46 Mu 3, Srisoonthorn Rd., Surin Beach, tel. 07/631-6500, www.twinpalms-phuket.com, 5,000B) is the perfect blend of urban chic and tropical resort. The guest rooms look out onto two big, beautiful pools and perfectly landscaped grounds, and inside is a blend of dark woods and clean whites—it's definitely designed for the jet-set crowd. What really makes the property stand out is the location. Though you could spend all your time lazing around the pool and eating at its restaurants, it's two minutes to the shore, and the resort has a small area reserved for guests, so you can enjoy comfortable chairs and great service on the beach, too.

KAMALA BEACH
Under 1,500B

The Print Kamala Resort (74/8 Mu 3, Kamala Beach, tel. 07/638-5396, www.print-kamalaresort.net, 1,400B), a few minutes by foot to Kamala Beach, is a good-value property for travelers who want to stay in a resort but don't want to pay five-star prices. Rooms have a neutral Thai decor and modern amenities but are a bit dated. The high density of rooms to common space and the fact that most rooms face the swimming pool mean you'll never feel total peace and quiet here, but the convenience the proximity to the beach

and to Kamala Village bring may make up for that fact.

1,500-3,000B

Kamala Dreams (96/42-74/1 Mu 3, Kamala Beach, tel. 07/627-9131, www.kamaladreams.net, 2,000B) is another good-value property if you are looking for a resort right on the beach. The property is very small—just under 20 rooms and suites—but there is a nice swimming pool and a restaurant on the premises. The rooms are large and come equipped with kitchenettes (microwaves and refrigerators) but are a little dated, as is the whole property. Kamala Village is directly behind Kamala Dreams, so there is plenty of eating and shopping close by.

Kamala Beach Resort—A Sunprime Resort (96/42-3 Mu 3, Kamala Beach, tel. 07/627-9580, www.kamalabeach.com, 2,700B) is a large, adults-only, midrange resort right on Kamala Beach. The massive common grounds have multiple swimming pools, bars, and restaurants, but if your room is at the far end of the resort, you'll be walking for a few minutes to get to the property's stretch of beach. Guest rooms are clean and modern and share the same subtle Thai style seen in most hotels in this price range. The decor isn't particularly charming, but it is inoffensive and practical. This is not a five-star luxury resort but has most high-end amenities, including minibars, satellite TV, and high-speed Internet in the guest rooms. No one under 15 is allowed at this resort.

Sunwing Resort Kamala Beach (96/66 Mu 3, Kamala Beach, tel. 07/637-1650, www.sunwingkamala.com, 2,700B) is a massive self-contained resort right in the center of Kamala Beach. Rooms are modern and comfortable, and even the smallest are designed with families in mind, as they have pull-out couches, refrigerators, and microwaves. The resort is full of families, so if the idea of kids running around is not appealing to you on vacation, look elsewhere! Those who have small kids will love the extensive activities for children, the waterslides, and the mascots that roam the grounds. For travelers looking for a one-stop shop, the resort has bars and restaurants on the premises, though it is so close to Kamala Village that it's easy to walk out to find other food and drink.

3,000-4,500B

Another great option for families is the Swissotel Phuket Kamala Beach (100/10 Mu 3, Kamala Beach, tel. 07/630-3000, www.swissotel.com, 3,200B), as the smallest rooms available are one-bedroom apartments with full living rooms and kitchenettes. All rooms overlook the large swimming pool in the center of the resort, and are modern and very large. Two-bedroom suites can be set up to accommodate families with children or groups of adults, and staff will bring in toys and play furniture as well. The kids' club has daily activities as well as a ball pit for children to play in. The only drawback is the fact that there is no direct beach access, guests must walk through an underpass to cross the road to get to Kamala Beach.

Over 4,500B

Set in the hills above Kamala Beach, the Paresa (49 Mu 6, Layi-Nakalay Rd., Kamala Beach, tel. 07/630-2000, www.paresaresorts.com, 20,000B) offers guests high-end, jet-set luxury in a convenient central location. The property's style—modern and minimalist—isn't oozing Thai character, but since the views of the island and the ocean are so stunning, guests won't be able to forget they are on Phuket. The large main infinity pool is set right in the cliffs over Kamala Beach. Villas and suites are spacious, and many have private pools as well as indoor and outdoor areas for entertaining.

PATONG BEACH
Under 1,500B

The Frutta Boutique Hotel Patong (86/14 Prabaramee Rd., Patong Beach, tel. 07/634-5092, www.frutta-boutique.com, 1,200B) is a fun, quirky little hotel with excellent-quality rooms and facilities for the money. The theme of the property is fruit, and every room and common space is decorated to embrace that theme. The result is colorful and playful; the rooms themselves are very clean and modern. There is a small, pretty swimming pool and a restaurant on the premises. Be warned that some of the cheaper rooms do not have windows.

Cheap and chic Me Hotel (39/119 Prabaramee Rd., Patong Beach, tel. 07/634-3044, 1,200B) has small, stylish guest rooms and very cheap prices. Beds are decked out with crisp white sheets and duvets, and the modern baths are equally minimalist and stylish. The lobby area is very small but so well decorated it looks totally out of place in the neighborhood. The downside is that you'll have to walk about 20 minutes to the beach (or take a taxi or *tuk tuk*), but for those who would rather save their money for martinis, it's not such a bad trade-off.

If you don't need a swimming pool or a gym, Patong Terrace (209-12/13 Rat-U-Thit 200 Pee Rd., Patong Beach, tel. 07/629-2159, www.patongterrace.com, 750B) is a good-value guesthouse in Patong. The modern decor is a nice change from the drab interiors that are so common among other guesthouses in this price range; bathrooms are much nicer than the competition. Located on a main road parallel to the beach road, the location is very central and can be loud at night, especially if your room faces the street. Service at this guesthouse is far better than most, and it tends to attract a loyal following of repeat customers.

YaYa Residence Phuket (187-187/1 Phra Bar Ram Mee Rd., Patong Beach, tel. 07/634-5191, www.yayaresidencephuket.com, 750B) is cheap, clean, and convenient. The guesthouse is on the northern end of Phuket, about 5 minutes on foot to the beach but about 20 minutes to the center of the nightlife scene. This is a good option if you're looking to save some cash and don't want to be in the middle of Patong.

The small, cheap, pleasant FunDee Boutique Hotel (232/3 Phung Muang Sai

Gor Rd., Patong Beach, tel. 07/636-6780, www.fundee.co.th, 1,200B) is a few blocks from Patong Beach but worth the walk if you're looking for something a little nicer than the average guesthouse. The property is only a few years old, spotlessly clean, and somewhat stylishly decorated with modern Thai furnishings and textiles. It's not really a boutique hotel and doesn't have a pool, but there is a very small bar and café as well as plenty of food and drink options just outside the door.

1,500-3,000B

ELLA Bed (100/19-20 Soi Perm Pong Pattana, Thawewong Rd., Patong Beach, tel. 07/634-4253, www.theellagroup.com, 2,200B) might be the most stylish small hotel in Patong. The industrial decor, which mixes carefully chosen furnishings with poured concrete and clean, white walls, is a refreshing break from the typical, play-it-safe decor in most hotels and resorts. Beach and bars are just a few minutes away on foot, but because ELLA Bed is tucked away in a side *soi*, it feels a little less hectic than the rest of Patong. There is a lovely café-bar on the first floor that's worth visiting even if you're not staying at the property. Service is great, too, and it's clear that the owner really cares about this place.

Salathai Resort Phuket (10/4 Sawasdirak Rd., Patong Beach, tel. 07/629-6631, www.phuketsalathai.com, 2,200B) is centrally located between Patong Beach and Jungceylon mall for those who want to enjoy the beach and the area's shopping and nightlife. Though it rates itself a three-star property, the fact that there is a decent swimming pool and a small restaurant-bar makes this resort more appealing than typical properties with that rating. Rooms are clean and comfortable, though the Thai-style decor seems a little dated. For the money, though, it would be hard to find a better property.

Over 4,500B

Holiday Inn Resort Patong (52 Taweewong Rd., Patong Beach, tel. 07/637-0200, www.ihg.com, 5,000B), on the southern part of Patong Beach, is a massive property with more than 400 guest rooms. Rooms, suites, and villas are tastefully decorated with subdued Thai accents, and the grounds are green and pretty. There are six swimming pools, and two restaurants and bars, though it's easy to get out to Patong from here, too. Families traveling together will appreciate the family suites, with multiple bedrooms and kitchenettes, as well as the kids' club and children's swimming pool.

A block in from the beach is The Nap Patong (5/55 Hat Patong Rd., Patong Beach, tel. 07/634-3111, www.thenappatong.com, 4,500B), a midsize, stylish boutique hotel. The minimalist design, with lots of stark white walls and poured concrete, is consistent throughout the guest rooms and the common areas, and although the property is only a four star, it does feel more upscale than most. The swimming pool is small, as are the rest of the facilities, though rooms are well sized considering the location.

If you want to enjoy ocean views but remove yourself from the hustle and bustle of Patong, consider the Senses Resort Patong (111/7 Nanai Rd., Patong Beach, tel. 07/633-6600, www.thesensesresort.com, 5,000B), located in the hills about a kilometer (0.6 mi) from the beach. Even basic rooms are spacious (over 500 square feet), and they are also tastefully fitted with sleek, modern furniture. The large infinity pool has a beautiful view of Patong below, and the property is designed in general to take advantage of the views and natural light. Though the property feels very grown-up, children are welcome and there is even a small kids' playroom.

KARON BEACH
Under 1,500B

A great budget option in Karon is the Pineapple Guesthouse (261/1 Patak Rd., Karon Plaza, tel. 07/639-6223, www.pineapplephuket.com, 700B), with very clean, basic guest rooms just a few minutes' walk from the beach. The outside is unimpressive and blends in with the overly aggressive signage in Karon

Plaza, but the owners have added some little extras inside, including colorful walls and decorations, to make the guest rooms stand out among so many competitors in the area. There are also shared dorms for those who want to save some cash or solo travelers looking to meet people.

1,500-3,000B

Simplitel Hotel (470/4 Patak Rd., Karon Beach, tel. 07/639-6531, www.simplitelphuket.com, 2,500B) offers modern, clean, comfortable hotel rooms in the middle of Karon Village. Aside from the nicely decorated rooms, the biggest draw here is the location, very convenient if you want to hang out at the beach during the day and go out in Karon Village at night. There is no swimming pool on this property, but the beach is walking distance away.

Sugar Palm Grand Hillside Resort (1 Soi Khoktanod Soi 3, Kata Rd., Karon Beach, tel. 07/633-0388, www.sugarpalmgrand.com, 2,500B) is a big, modern, attractive resort in the hills above Kata and Karon Beaches. Chic European-style rooms are large (standard ones start at about 450 square feet), and many have nice views of the surrounding hills. The infinity swimming pool, which cascades down in a series of steps, is very cool, and there is a fitness room and spa on the premises. This property is just a few minutes on foot to Kata and Karon Villages.

Kanita Resort & Camping (23/2 Soi Patak, Karon Beach, tel. 07/651-0233, www.phuketkanita.com, 1,500B) offers guests a more secluded, less urban location than most places in Karon, plus modern, new rooms (the resort opened in 2013) and even camping facilities. There is a small swimming pool and restaurant on the premises, too. The lush grounds, and surrounding neighborhood, will let you enjoy the natural beauty of Phuket, but the downside is that it is a very long walk to the beach and a tougher walk back, as the resort is in the hills.

3,000-4,500B

Phunawa Resort (16/1 Patak Rd. Soi 24, Karon Beach, tel. 07/636-3000, www.phunawa.com, 3,500B) is an all-suites resort with large one- and two-bedroom suites, perfect for families, groups, or those staying for long stretches of time. Larger suites have full kitchens instead of kitchenettes. Inside, rooms are modern and very bright, with light furniture and textiles. The large, circular pool, around which most guest suites are located, makes up for the fact that the grounds are not extensive. The resort is in the Karon hills, close enough to walk for those in good shape and if the weather isn't too hot, but otherwise you'll need to arrange transport through the resort or on your own.

Mandarava Resort and Spa (14/2 Patak Rd. Soi 24, Karon Beach, tel. 07/668-1800, www.mandavaresort.com, 3,500B) is a beautiful, modern, Thai-style resort in the hills of Karon. Rooms, suites, and villas are big and comfortable, and decor is subdued and modern. As the property is in the hills, the three swimming pools and various decks scattered throughout the property really take advantage of the views. The resort has dining and drinking options, but if you want to go into town you'll have to take the free shuttle or arrange other transportation, as it's just too far to walk comfortably. Children under 12 are not allowed at the Mandarava Resort and Spa.

Over 4,500B

Centara Grand Beach Resort Phuket (683 Patak Rd., Karon Beach, tel. 07/620-1234, www.centarahotelsresorts.com, 5,500B) has every amenity and facility one could possibly want on vacation—restaurants, bars, a fitness center, multiple swimming pools, waterslides and a lazy river worthy of a water park, a kids' club, a fancy spa, the list goes on. It's also right on the beach, so you could arrive at the Centara, unpack your bags, and never leave the resort for your whole vacation. If you do want to venture out, though, you are right near the center of the action and can get to Patong in 10 minutes or Karon Village in just a few. Though most large resorts offer good buffet breakfasts, the Centara's is just a little bigger and a little better. A great choice for families, though you will pay for all the amenities and conveniences. During high season, though, this resort can be very crowded.

Le Meridien Phuket Beach Resort (29 Soi Karon Nui, Karon Beach, tel. 07/637-0100, www.lemeridienphuketbeachresort.com, 6,500B) is one of the best-located resorts in all of Phuket. It's on a small stretch of beach in northern Karon, and though it technically isn't private, as there's nothing on either side and limited access, there are few people other than guests and hotel employees around. Like the Centara Grand, it's also very close to Karon and Patong, so you won't spend too much time or money getting out if you want to. Amenities and facilities are excellent, with multiple restaurants, a massive swimming pool, a kids' club and large outdoor playground, and a spa. Most guest rooms have been recently renovated and are simple and modern with some Thai decor. With almost 500 rooms, this is a very large property, but service still feels personal and friendly.

KATA BEACH
Under 1,500B

Waree's Guesthouse (40 Patak Rd. Soi 7, Karon Beach, tel. 07/633-1016, 1,200B) is a basic, old-fashioned guesthouse with comfortable, clean rooms and a small but pleasant garden area. With just a handful of rooms, service at this family-run property is very personal, and it tends to attract repeat visitors. The residential neighborhood this guesthouse is located in is about 10 minutes from the beach.

Eazy Resort (64/22-37 Kata Rd., Kata Beach, tel. 07/628-4401, www.eazyresort.com, 1,200B) has everything a traveler needs—clean rooms, a swimming pool, a small restaurant, and a good location within walking distance of the beach. It opened in 2013, so everything is new and in good repair. Eazy Resort really is more a motel than a resort,

though, and the only grounds to speak of are the swimming pool and the restaurant.

Kata High View Resort (233 Koketanode Rd., Kata, tel. 07/633-0660, www.katahiviewresort.com, 1,200B) is a lovely, inexpensive small resort with a nice swimming pool, modern, well-designed rooms, and a location about 10 minutes on foot from Kata Beach. This is a budget property, and there is no restaurant on the premises, not too much of a problem as it is so close to Kata Village and all the food and drink offerings there. The resort is set in the hills above Kata, which makes for great views from some of the common areas. You'll need to climb up stairs to get to your room, though, which would be challenging for small children or anyone with limited mobility.

1,500-3,000B

The Palmery Resort and Spa (82/20 Koketanode Rd., Kata Beach, tel. 07/633-3171, www.thepalmery.com, 2,200B) is a good-value resort in the hills behind Kata Beach. The property, which opened in 2013, has spacious rooms that are comfortably equipped. The clean, modern design of this midsize resort seems to appeal to younger couples, which seems to be the biggest demographic at the resort. Like most resorts of this size, the "heart" of the property is the swimming pool, in this case a sleek, minimalist one with pretty blue tiles.

Some may find the overt Thai decor at Sawasdee Village (65 Katekwan Rd., Kata Beach, tel. 07/633-0979, www.phuketsawasdee.com, 3,000B) a bit over the top, but once inside this small, upscale resort, most suspend their cynicism and embrace it for what it is. In fact, many find that the lush landscaping, Khmer-style architecture, and regional art that decorates Sawasdee Village create a beautiful, exotic environment. Aside from aesthetics, the resort has plenty going for it. Service at the resort is very friendly, and the location can't be beat—it's about 150 meters (492 ft) from the beach, and Kata Village is at its doorstep.

Aspasia Resort (1/3 Laem Sai Rd., Kata Beach, tel. 07/628-4430, www.aspasiaphuket.com, 2,900B) isn't quite a five-star luxury resort, but it offers guests an experience that comes quite close, for a much lower price. The location in the hills between Karon and Kata Beaches, overlooking the water, feels remote and secluded but is in fact very central. The rooms have a modern Asian aesthetic, with simple but high-end wooden furniture. Large suites with full kitchens are great for long stays and big groups. The stepped grounds are lovely, though they might not be that suitable for families with small children.

3,000-4,500B

Metadee Resort (66 Kata Rd., Kata Beach, tel. 07/633-7888, www.metadeephuket.com, 3,500B), a modern, full-service resort a 10-minute walk from the beach, has a stunning, massive, free-form central swimming pool. The modern, spacious villas and guest rooms are clustered around the pool, and some have direct access from their balconies, though some have their own smaller, private pools. The overall design at the resort is clean, light, and minimalist, with some small Thai details. There is a fitness center, a spa, and a restaurant on the premises, and it's just a short walk to town. This is not quite a five-star property, but if you're able to book it at a discount, it's a great value in a great location.

For a larger family-friendly property near Kata Beach, try Kata Palm Resort (60 Kata Rd., Karon, tel. 07/628-4334, www.katapalm-resort.com, 3,500B). The resort is just a few minutes on foot to Kata Beach but also has a very large pool area with a funky little artificial waterfall and a bar in one of the pools, should you wish to remain at the resort for the day. Guest rooms are a mix of traditional Thai with a nondescript large hotel; it's nothing stunning from a design point of view but definitely nice-looking, clean, and comfortable.

Over 4,500B

Boathouse by Montara (Kata Beach, tel. 07/633-0015 to 07/633-0017, www.boathousephuket.com, 6,500B), formerly called Mom Tri's Boathouse, is a beautiful small hotel in a fantastic spot right at the end of Kata Beach. The comfortably appointed guest rooms are decorated in a modern Thai style, and many have views looking right out onto the ocean. After extensive renovations in 2012, the property feels fresh and modern. There is an excellent restaurant on the premises, and a spa and small swimming pool, too. This is a great place to stay if you're looking for something a little more upscale right on Kata Beach.

Perhaps one of the highest-rated resorts on Kata Beach, by any standard, is Mom Tri's Villa Royale (12 Kata Noi Rd., Kata Beach, tel. 07/633-3586, www.villaroyalephuket.com, 9,500B). Set on Kata Noi, the resort scales the cliffs behind the shore. All rooms and suites are very large and include sitting areas. Decor is very low-key and elegant—clearly the architect who designed and owns this property didn't want to compete with the gorgeous natural surroundings. With just 35 rooms and suites, the resort is very small, and the service level is very high. Though the resort is very close to everything going on in Kata and Karon, the premises feels very private and secluded, a real luxury in Phuket.

NAI HARN

The Royal Phuket Yacht Club (23/3 Mu 1, Viset Rd., Nai Harn, tel. 07/638-0200, www.theroyalphuketyachtclub.com, 4,000B) on Nai Harn Beach is a well-established, large luxury resort with beautiful views of the Andaman Sea, nice facilities, and comfortable rooms. The facilities and common areas are pretty and well designed, with the large swimming pool overlooking the ocean. The property underwent renovations in 2014.

The very popular U Sunsiri Phuket (11/5 Mu 1, Rawai, tel. 07/633-6400, www.uhotelsresorts.com, 3,000B) resort, a few hundred meters inland from Nai Harn Beach, opened in 2013. The eclectic design choices—a bit of industrial chic, some Asian furnishings, and even some old-world opulence—come together to create a very modern, aesthetically pleasing resort. The kids' club and waterslide make this a family-friendly property, as do the large suites with kitchenettes. As for food and drink, the hotel has multiple bars and restaurants, but you can also walk out to the beach for inexpensive Thai and Western food.

RAWAI BEACH

Le Piman Resort (43/148 Mu 7, Viset Rd., Rawai, tel. 07/661-3732, www.lepimanresort. com, 1,500B) is a nice small midmarket resort and a good value for those who want to stay in the area. The very pretty grounds, comfortable villas and guest rooms, and friendly service almost make up for the fact that the property isn't near any swimmable beaches, though that's a problem in all of Rawai.

Navatara Phuket Resort (90/28 Mu 6, Viset Rd., Rawai, tel. 07/661-3879, www.navataresort.com, 1,500B) is another great property on the wrong side of the tracks. The small resort, centered on a wide, pretty swimming pool, designed with subtle Thai architectural elements, is pretty and neutral. Basic rooms are comfortably sized at around 350 square feet and are modern and fitted with everything from hair dryers to Wi-Fi. There's nothing to speak of in the area, though the resort provides a free shuttle bus to nearby attractions.

Serenity Resort and Residences Phuket (14 Mu 5, Viset Rd., Rawai, tel. 07/637-1900, www.serenityphuket.com, 3,000B), a midsize luxury resort on the coast of Rawai Beach, has comfortable, modern rooms and some very large suites for families and large groups. The small island of Ko Lon is directly across the water from the resort, making for a beautiful view. You can kayak and do other ocean activities. The beach itself is not swimmable or fit for sunbathing, though; it's essentially a tidal mud flat.

PHUKET TOWN

If there ever was a reason to stay in Phuket Town, it would have to be Phuket 346 (15 Soi Romanee, Thalang Rd., Phuket Town, tel. 07/625-8108, www.phuket346.com, 1,300B),

an art gallery-guesthouse in an old Sino-Portuguese shophouse in the center of the city. Each of Phuket 346's three guest rooms are quirky and funky but have big, comfortable beds, TVs, and Wi-Fi. The lobby, gallery, and attached café are very modern but have incorporated Phuket Town's historic architecture.

99 Oldtown Boutique Guesthouse (99 Thalang Rd., Phuket Town, tel. 081/797-4311, 800B) is another wonderful place to stay in Phuket Town. The perfect location in the center of the historic district, charming, authentic rooms, and very modern bathrooms mean you'll be talking about this place long after you head home from Phuket. The price, less than US$25 per night most times of the year, is unbeatable for what you get.

More of a hostel than a guesthouse or hotel, Ai Phuket (88 Yawolat Rd., Phuket Town, www.aiphukethostel.com, tel. 081/721-2881, 300B) is cheap, clean, and fun, plus it's in a historic Sino-Portuguese building in the center of town. Shared dorm rooms have a typical bunk bed setup, but they are very colorful and well decorated, a surprise at this price range. Shared bathrooms are modern and very cool, nothing like the typical hostel. The lobby and other common areas are also filled with funky art and comfortable places to sit and read.

NEARBY ISLANDS

Coral Island Resort (Coral Island, tel. 07/628-1060, www.coralislandresort.com, 2,500B) is the only option you have if you want to stay on this beautiful little island just off Phuket. The resort is basic, with decent but aging rooms, a restaurant, and even a swimming pool, but the reason people come here is not for the accommodations so much as the island itself. If you're interested in snorkeling or diving off Coral Island, adjust your expectations for this resort, relish in the fact that it's so inexpensive for the location, and enjoy your trip.

Bungalow Raya Resort (Ko Racha, tel. 07/638-3136, www.rayaresort.net, 1,200B) has basic, old-fashioned beach bungalows on Ko

Racha. Fan cooling, cold water, and basic bedding are on offer, but even if you're past your backpacking days, the location overlooking the beach is worth any amount of inconvenience or discomfort. There is also a small restaurant-bar on the premises.

The Racha Phuket Resort (Ko Racha, tel. 07/635-5455, www.theracha.com, 7,000B) is a small five-star luxury resort on the secluded island of Ko Racha. Stark white interiors and minimalist, Mediterranean-inspired design make the resort feel very modern inside and out. The large central swimming pool overlooks the ocean, and the resort itself is just steps away from the sand. Day-trippers, though, can make the beach feel crowded and hectic, so it's best to spend your time there in the early morning or late afternoon.

Tenta Nakara Resort (31/1 Mu 5, Ko Naka Yai, tel. 081/398-6515, www.tentanakara.com, 1,700B) is all about getting back to nature. There's no electricity, and the old-fashioned thatched-roof bungalows and tents are designed to remove as many barriers to the outdoors as possible. It's not all about roughing it, though, as bathrooms are modern and there is even a small place to get massages on the premises. The restaurant on the premises runs on generator power in the evening, but things shut down pretty early here, so don't expect a big party. Large, multibedroom bungalows are very family-friendly, too.

The Naka Island (32 Mu 5, Ko Naka Yai, tel. 07/637-1400, www.nakaislandphuket.com, 13,000B), part of the Starwoods Luxury Collection, is an all-villa property on a semi-private stretch of beach on Ko Naka Yai. Even basic villas are over 4,000 square feet and have small private plunge pools. The decor is very tropical, with thatched roofs, adobe-like structures, and plenty of natural materials. The main swimming pool has a beautiful view of Phang Nga Bay. There are two restaurants and a bar, though you may feel a little captive to the (expensive) food and drinks on offer. The resort includes pickup from the airport and transfer to the island by private boat; it's a very exciting and exclusive experience.

Food

You'll find that although the island is packed full of beautiful resorts and beaches, food offerings are simply not up to par with what you'll find in Bangkok and other urban areas in the country. Things are definitely improving, and there are some great restaurants on Phuket, though. Many restaurants in tourist areas offer some sort of hybrid menu combining Thai food and Western food, whether it's German, French, Italian, Swiss, or just cheeseburgers and french fries to go with your pad thai or fried rice. Unfortunately, most places do neither cuisine particularly well but manage to stay in business because they're located on the beach or because visitors are happy enough to be in such beautiful surroundings that they're not so bothered by the lack of excellent food. Though hotel restaurants are usually less interesting than stand-alone ones, on Phuket they are often where you will find the best meals (casual Thai food excepted).

MAI KHAO BEACH

Kin Dee Restaurant (71/6 Mai Khao Beach, tel. 082/814-8482, 10:30am-10pm daily, 100B), a beach restaurant serving good Thai food, has become a favorite among tourists in Mai Khao. The relaxed atmosphere, inexpensive prices, and friendly service make it a really pleasant experience. This is a very casual place—just an open-air dining area filled with bamboo furniture. They also deliver and even have a Thai cooking class.

The comfortable but modern and stylish

dining room at Cinnamon (53/3-4 Mu 4, Mai Khao, tel. 07/661-6253, 11am-11pm Wed.-Mon., 300B) serves good, straightforward Thai dishes plus pasta and sandwiches. Though it is out of the way if you're not staying in the area, if you're at a nearby resort it's worth the trip for a little change of scenery.

NAI YANG BEACH

Tatonka (382/19 Mu 1, Srisoontorn Rd., Cherngtalay, Thalang, tel. 07/632-4399, 6pm-midnight Thurs.-Tues., 600B) just outside of the Laguna Resort area, offers innovative global cuisine in a Native American-themed restaurant with an open kitchen where you can watch chefs prepare your Thai bouillabaisse or Peking duck pizza. This is some of the best fusion food you'll find on the island, and the dining room and outdoor dining areas have a casual elegance to them.

The attractive, high-end Thai@Siam (82/17 Mu 5, Nai Yang Beach, tel. 07/632-8290, 11:30am-11pm daily, 450B) features mostly Thai seafood dishes served in a lovely setting—an expansive old wooden Thai house surrounded by lush gardens. In addition to Thai classics such as fried spring rolls and *yam talay* (seafood salad), there are also some Western dishes and fusion dishes. This is really a restaurant for travelers, so those who want more intense flavors should make that clear when ordering.

The casual but sophisticated Siam Supper Club (36/40 Lagoon Rd., Cherntalay, tel. 07/627-0936, 11:30am-6pm daily, 800B) serves a high-end, European-heavy menu with some local cuisine. The atmosphere, reminiscent of an old speakeasy, is even more convincing when there is live jazz music playing (call for the schedule). Even without live music, this place exudes the type of sophisticated charm you rarely see on a tropical island. Prices, especially for imported wines, can be quite high, but many visitors find it a worthwhile splurge.

SURIN BEACH

Right on Surin Beach, there are a number of small restaurants serving up seaside meals and offering menus of both Thai and Western food. Everything is pretty much predictably decent and inexpensive. If you come around dusk and sit at one of the tables on the beach, you'll feel like you're dining like royalty regardless of what you're eating—the view from the tables is magnificent during sunset. In the parking lot of the beach, a number of street vendors begin setting up in the late afternoon, and there is plenty to choose from there if you're looking for something more casual.

Twin Brothers (Surin Beach, tel. 09/591-1274, 11am-10pm daily, 200B) is a little fancier than most of the choices on the beach. They have a mixed Thai and Western menu, including pizza. In addition to the food, they've set up a free Wi-Fi zone, so you can surf the Net and eat at the same time.

For something a little more upscale right on the beach, ★ Catch Beach Club (Surin Beach, directly across from Twin Palms, tel. 07/631-6500, 11am-11pm daily, 500B), the beach restaurant of the Twin Palms, has indoor and outdoor seating that opens right onto the beach. The restaurant, done in stark white with an amazing array of cocktails and a good wine list, is more Miami Beach than Surin. They also have live-music performances on the weekends. It's a jet-set spot on an otherwise totally unpretentious beach. But despite appearances, it is a laid-back and friendly place to have food or drinks.

In keeping with the upscale urban trendiness that characterizes many of the best resorts in Surin, Kindee (71/6 Mu 5, Mai Khao Beach, tel. 07/634-8478, www.kindeerestaurant.com, noon-11pm daily, 250B) offers authentic, flavorful Thai dishes in an unpretentious, relaxed outdoor restaurant. The atmosphere, basic bamboo furniture in lush surroundings, is casual but very pretty. The vast menu includes familiar dishes such as pad thai and some, such as banana flower salad, that new visitors to Thailand may not have tried before. The owner also offers cooking classes.

KAMALA BEACH

At the southern end of Kamala Beach is ★ Rockfish (33/6 Kamala Beach Rd., tel. 07/627-9732, 8am-10pm daily, 500B), one of the most popular restaurants on the islands. No wonder it gets kudos: The menu, split into Thai, Western, and fusion sections, has something for everyone but does everything well, apparently a difficult task considering the quality of fare served up at many tourist-oriented restaurants in the area. The restaurant-bar also has a nice casual atmosphere and, set right on the beach, a beautiful view of the Andaman Sea.

White Orchid (18/40 Mu 6, Kamala Beach, tel. 08/1892-9757, 11:30am-11pm daily, 250B) offers inexpensive but well-prepared classic Thai dishes in a pleasant setting on the beach. The restaurant, essentially a large thatched-roof roadside shack on Kamala Beach, also has tables on the sand. Service is very friendly and relaxed. Eating here feels a little like Phuket used to be—full of character and less crowded and commercialized.

★ Silk (Andara Resort and Villas, 15 Mu 6, Kamala Beach, tel. 07/633-8777, www.silk-phuket.com, 6pm-1am daily, 600B) recently relocated from its Surin Plaza location to more central Kamala Beach, but it's still as swanky and chic as ever. No wonder: It's owned by the same group that owns the popular bar area Lan Kwai Fong in Hong Kong. The interior is stunning, with soaring ceilings, red silk, and dark wood throughout, and you can have your meal served at one of the dining tables or, if you're feeling indulgent, lounging on one of the opium beds. The menu has many typical Thai dishes with a little extra flair, such as the panang curry with duck and asparagus.

PATONG BEACH

Patong Beach has everything, and lots of it. Hundreds of guesthouses, hotels, and resorts, hundreds of little shops to spend your money in, and hundreds of places—from small street stalls to sit-down restaurants and familiar Western-brand fast food—to find something to eat. Quantity aside, Patong is unfortunately not known for quality dining. To find the best places, you'll have to venture out a little bit. If you're looking for some authentic Thai food and are not too picky about where you eat, venture over to the night market on Rat-U-Thit Road, parallel to the beach, between Soi Bangla and Sawatdirak Road. You'll find plenty of seafood and other stalls set up, catering to hungry visitors and locals alike.

Right in the center of all the action, across the street from the beach, is the Ban Thai Restaurant (94 Thaveewong Rd., Patong Beach, tel. 07/634-0850, 11am-1am daily, 500B). The outdoor dining area is lovelier than one would expect in the middle of Patong Beach, and the seafood is fresh and well prepared. The restaurant is great for people-watching, but it's not a place for a quiet romantic dinner: There's often loud live music playing in the background and plenty of commotion to be heard from the streets of Patong.

Unpretentiously serving up solid Thai food, Kaab Gluay (58/3 Phrabaramee Rd., Patong Beach, tel. 07/634-0562, 5am-2:30pm daily, 200B) is always a favorite among local residents. The simple restaurant up the road from Patong Beach has many of the Thai dishes you'll see all over the country, including *tom yam kung,* but also fresh local fish dishes, all for very reasonable prices.

An excellent choice for high Thai cuisine is Baan Rim Pa (223 Prabaramee Rd., Patong, tel. 07/634-0789, noon-10pm daily, 600B), in the cliffs adjacent to Patong Beach, overlooking the ocean. The view is wonderful, and the food is solid, although the menu may feel a little touristy. The atmosphere is relaxed but much more formal than most beachfront restaurants. It's not the type of place to walk into in flip-flops after a day at the beach, but it's a great choice for a special night out on the island.

If you're in the mood for Indian, Navrang Mahal (58/11 Bangla Rd., Soi Patong Resort, tel. 07/629-2280, noon-midnight daily, 300B) off Soi Bangla is unpretentious and relaxed but has fantastic food. They have both northern and southern dishes on the menu, and you'll find good curries and dals as well as many dishes with fresh seafood.

Another excellent Indian choice is Tantra (186/5-6 Taweewong Rd., tel. 07/629-6016, noon-midnight daily, 300B), right on the main beach road. The modern Indian decor feels very loungy, helped by the floor seating. The menu is unsurprising, but it includes favorites such as tandoori chicken, saag paneer, and samosas.

For something a little more chic, with a great view and a relaxed vibe, ★ Joe's Downstairs (223 Prabaramee Rd., Patong, tel. 07/634-4254, noon-1am daily, 600B), right below Baan Rim Pa, is a fun tapas bar-cocktail lounge-restaurant with an international menu. The modern white interior is a nice backdrop to the view of the ocean and the colorful, artfully arranged dishes.

White Box (247/5 Prabaramee Rd., Kalim Beach, Patong, tel. 07/634-6271, noon-11pm daily, 800B), a slick modern restaurant just north of Patong Beach on the beach side, has great views of the ocean from the glass-enclosed indoor dining room or the terrace. The trendy restaurant's menu, which includes French, Thai, and fusion dishes, is a bit pricey, but the atmosphere, views, and attentive service make it worth the price. Those who don't want to dine here can stop in for rooftop cocktails and live jazz instead.

Sure, you're not in Cabo, but if you're in the mood for some Mexican food, head to Coyote (94 Beach Rd., Patong Beach, tel. 07/634-4366, 11:30am-11pm daily, 350B) on Patong. Like their locations in Bangkok, the decor is bright and colorful, the margarita menu huge, and the food surprisingly good considering how far you are from Mexico.

KARON BEACH AND KATA BEACH

Karon and Kata, listed together because the two villages are connected, have a great variety of food and drink options within walking distance of the beach, one of the reasons the area is such a popular place to stay. For high-end dining, stick with one of the resort restaurants, as there are so far no excellent stand-alone restaurants in the area. But, for casual lunches and dinners, there are plenty of options.

The Kata Night Plaza (100 Rd., Kata Beach, Kata, tel. 080/087-3475, hours vary), a small outdoor mall that opened in 2013, has a number of restaurants, including a pizza place, La Piazzetta, a sushi restaurant, Big Fish, and a few other small places to eat. It also has a number of chain restaurants, including a Pizza Company, a Coffee Club, a Swensen's, and a Wine Connection.

Set inside the Aspasia Phuket, Malina's (1/3 Laem Sai Rd., Kata Beach, Karon, tel. 07/633-3033, 7am-11pm daily, 500B) has a chic contemporary feeling thanks to lots of stainless steel and glass, and it offers a Thai menu as well as Mediterranean fare. The food is less edgy than the decor, but expect the Thai dishes, such as seafood in tamarind soup, to be more interpretive than what you'll find at traditional restaurants. The best part of the place, aside from the view to the sea from outdoor seats, is the desserts.

The Boathouse (Kata Beach, tel. 07/633-0015, www.boathousephuket.com, 10:30am-11pm daily, 800B), right on Kata Beach, is the restaurant next to Mom Tri's and has one of the best wine selections on the island. This is definitely a place to trade the flip-flops for nicer garb. The kitchen serves both Thai and Western food, and although the restaurant is technically indoors, it opens out onto the beach, and there's a wonderful view to accompany your meal.

Locanda (Bougainvillea Terrace Resort, 86 Patak Rd., Kata Beach, tel. 07/633-0139, www.locanda-phuket.com, 2pm-2am daily, 1,000B) in Kata is part Argentinean churrascaria, part Thai restaurant that is owned by Swiss people and has an Italian name, but the combination works well. It's one of the best places on the island to get a steak. A big plus for those balking at the sorry selection of wines on the island, there's also a wine cellar with Old World and New World wines to choose from. If you're not totally stuffed by the grilled meats, the restaurant has a small but well-prepared Thai menu.

The entrance to Kampong Kata Hill (4 Karon Rd., Kata, tel. 07/633-0103, 6pm-11pm daily, 500B), in the center of Kata, is easy to miss, but if you walk up the hill on the (many) outdoor stairs, you'll find one of the nicest Thai restaurants in the area. The decor, filled with Thai antiques and Buddha images, might seem a bit over-the-top to some, but it's pretty and pleasant. The menu includes just about every Thai dish imaginable, from Thai salads to curries plus plenty of seafood.

Two Chefs Bar and Grill (526/7-8 Patak Rd., Karon Beach, tel. 07/628-6479, www. twochefs-phuket.com, 8am-11pm daily, 450B) probably comes the closest to American chain-restaurant dining on Phuket. The restaurant serves a mixed menu of Tex-Mex, Thai food, sandwiches, and burgers in a comfortable, modern setting. Though the Thai food is definitely toned down for Western palates, it's consistent, and most find the flavors plenty intense. They also serve some hearty breakfast dishes in the morning. In addition to the Karon location, there are two locations in Kata.

Old Siam Restaurant (Thavorn Palm Beach Resort, 311 Patak Rd., Karon Beach, tel. 07/639-6090, www.thavornpalmbeach.com, noon-10:30pm daily, 650B) in the Thavorn Palm Beach Resort, has good Thai food, including the usual *tom yam kung* and Thai curries, but the location, an outdoor dining room with views of the beach, makes it worth visiting. It's more casual than some of the other, higher-end hotel restaurants.

PHUKET TOWN

The night market in Phuket Town, on Ong Sim Fai Road near the bus station, probably has the best casual food in the vicinity. Although Phuket Town attracts a number of travelers, the diners here are mostly locals,

and the food is consequently reasonably priced and freshly prepared.

Phuket Town's historic center has a handful of lovely cafés. ★ Kopitiam by Wilai (18 Thalang Rd., Phuket Town, tel. 083/606-9776, 11am-10pm daily, 300B) might not be the chicest or most modern, but it's a contender for most interesting. The little café is filled with cool photos of Phuket from decades past, and the old Chinese furnishings and decorations are that much more convincing given the old Thai-Chinese men that hang out here on occasion. Aside from coffee, Malaysian-style tea, and snacks, there is also a full lunch and dinner menu.

★ Raya Thai (48 Deebuk Rd., Phuket Town, tel. 07/621-8155, 10am-11pm daily, 300B) is a must if you're anywhere near Phuket Town around lunch or dinnertime and prefer excellent local food and charming atmosphere to Westernized menus and slick decor. The elegant yet unpretentious restaurant is in an old Chinese-style home, and there's also outdoor seating in the small courtyard. Madam Rose (as the restaurant is sometimes called) has been running things for decades, and she offers deliciously prepared traditional Thai cuisine, with lots of fresh seafood on the menu. The *tom yam kung* is particularly good. This is one of those gems that's more popular with out-of-town Thais on vacation than with hordes of Westerners. It is a very family-friendly restaurant, too.

Even if you're not staying in Phuket Town, Siam Indigo Bar & Restaurant (8 Phang Nga Rd., Phuket Town, tel. 07/625-6697, www.siamindigo.com, 6:30am-11pm daily, 500B) is reason enough to make the trip. The restaurant, set in a nicely restored old Sino-Portuguese building, offers a mixed menu of Thai and French fusion dishes as well as creative cocktails. The decor is fresh and modern, and the space also doubles as a modern art gallery to showcase local artists' work.

The stately, expansive Baan Klung Jinda Restaurant (158 Yaowarat Rd., Phuket Town, tel. 07/622-1777, 11am-2pm and 5pm-10pm Mon.-Sat., 350B) is set in an old colonial-style house, complete with porticos and shuttered windows, a definite step up from most of the dining options on the island. Inside, the menu is deliberately traditional and typical, although there are some more exotic ingredients such as venison. Expect to find lots of curry and seafood dishes, all well prepared and presented. The restaurant also has a good wine selection, another plus if you're looking for a special place to dine.

Blue Elephant Cooking School and Restaurant (96 Krabi Rd., Phuket Town, tel. 07/635-4355, 11:30am-10:30pm daily, 650B), set in the old Phuket governor's mansion, has been serving royal Thai cuisine to patrons for years. Dishes, including curries and *tom yam kung,* will seem familiar to most who know Thai food, but presentation here is meticulous. The physical setting, another old colonial mansion, is stunning and makes for a very special spot for lunch or dinner. Like the Bangkok location, the Blue Elephant in Phuket also offers cooking classes.

La Gaetana (352 Phuket Rd., Phuket Town, tel. 07/625-0523, 6pm-11pm Thurs.-Tues., 700B) offers classic Italian cooking in a homey, friendly environment in Phuket Town. The full menu includes antipasti, pastas, meat dishes, and some yummy Italian desserts. The owner is around most nights, and service can be a bit stereotypically attentive, though from the reactions of diners most seem to enjoy it. Make sure to book for dinner as the place can fill up.

Another European favorite in Phuket Town is Brasserie Phuket (18 Rassada Rd., Phuket Town, tel. 07/621-0511, 11am-midnight daily, 1,100B), a Belgian restaurant with a seafood-heavy menu and imported Belgian beers. The dining room is pretty and modern, though perhaps not as opulent as you'd expect given the prices, which can be high. Still, the fresh seafood, including lots of salmon and even fresh oysters, are worth it and at such high quality are hard to find in Phuket.

There are several seafood restaurants along Chalong Bay, but Kan-Eang Seafood (9/3 Chofa Rd., Chalong Bay, tel. 07/638-1323, 10am-midnight daily, 400B) is a favorite among returning visitors to the island. Originally opened in the 1970s as a small fish stand, Kan-Eang has grown into a large open-air restaurant facing the bay. Try the steamed fish with lime and chili sauce and crab-fried rice for an authentic local seafood meal. This restaurant is insanely popular with large tour groups, but don't be put off by the big buses in the parking lot.

Wood-fired pizza, fresh seafood, Thai food, and a great view are what draw travelers and expats to Nikita's (Rawai Beach Rd., tel. 07/628-8703, 10am-1am daily, 250B) night after night. You might not get that cultural experience you've been craving if you come for dinner, but you'll definitely satisfy any pizza urges. The view from the tables on Rawai beach, the cold beer on tap, and the relaxed atmosphere only add to the experience.

Information and Services

TOURIST AND TRAVEL INFORMATION

The main island tourist office (191 Thalang Rd., Phuket Town, tel. 07/621-2213 or 07/621-1036, www.tourismthailand.org) is located in Phuket Town and offers maps and general information about the island. There's also a Tourism Authority of Thailand office right in the airport, and it's a convenient place to grab some maps and get general information.

There is also a noticeable presence of

tourist police in Phuket, especially during the high season. If there's ever a need, dial tel. 02/678-6800, 02/678-6809, or toll-free 1699 from any phone in Thailand.

BANKS AND CURRENCY EXCHANGE

As long as your local bank is on one of the international networks, such as Cirrus, you should have no problems getting access to money anywhere on Phuket, although some of the outlying islands don't have ATMs or banks. There are ATMs and currency-exchange kiosks in the Phuket International Airport.

You will get the best rate if you use your ATM card instead of changing currency or travelers checks, but all Thai banks charge a 180 baht fee in addition to any fee your own bank may charge, so you have to factor that in when deciding on the best way to handle your money (they also charge a 150 baht fee to cash travelers checks, so it may be a wash). Thai ATMs all have an English-language option. Remember that Phuket is a pretty casual place, and you'll most likely be spending a lot of time swimming, away from your valuables, or on a boat with other travelers you don't know, so it's better not to carry wads of cash with you. If your hotel doesn't have a safe that you feel confident with (and most casual bungalows don't), take out only as much money as you need for a day or two.

Branches of all of the major banks offer currency-exchange services in Phuket Town, Patong, and the other large beach areas. Rates are always posted, and after you calculate in fees and commissions, they will be better than anything you'll get from someone offering to exchange money for you on the street or out of a shop front. You may be required to show your passport, so make sure to bring it with you. If you want to exchange travelers checks, you will be able to do so at any of the bank branches as well.

International hotels and restaurants will take American Express, MasterCard, and Visa cards, but smaller guesthouses and virtually all casual restaurants are cash-only. You may be asked to pay an additional fee, usually 2-3 percent, to use a credit card. Though all major credit card companies prohibit the practice, it's rampant in Thailand.

EMERGENCY AND MEDICAL SERVICES

Phuket has two major private hospitals with English-speaking staff. While the level of service may not be as high as in the swanky international hospitals in Bangkok, these institutions do cater to foreigners, and staff are well trained and professional. If there is an emergency or you need to be seen by a doctor before you head off the island, do not hesitate to stop into one of these hospitals. Both have 24-hour walk-in services for a fraction of what you'd pay back home. Bangkok Hospital Phuket (2/1 Hongyok Utis Rd., Phuket Town, tel. 07/625-4425) is located in Phuket Town. Phuket International Hospital (44 Chalermprakiat Ror 9 Rd., tel. 07/624-9400) is on the airport bypass road. Both hospitals have emergency services. If you want help from Bangkok Hospital, dial 1719 from any local phone. The Bangkok Hospital has a 24-hour emergency response, including ambulance service. The emergency number for Phuket International Hospital is 07/621-0935, and they also have 24-hour emergency service. If you are using Phuket as a base and heading out to one of the surrounding islands, remember that you may be hours away from medical care.

There are small pharmacies all over the island if you need medications, many of which are available here without a prescription, though if you need something that isn't commonly used in Thailand, you may have trouble getting it. Antibiotics and oral contraceptives are very easy to find, but make sure you know the generic name of the drug you need, as many pharmaceutical companies brand their products differently in different countries.

VISAS AND OFFICIALDOM

Neither the American embassy (tel. 02/205-4000), the British embassy (tel. 08/1854-7362), nor the Australian embassy (tel. 02/344-6300) has a consular office on the island, but each can be reached by phone in case of emergency or to provide guidance.

COMMUNICATIONS

The best place to get stamps is at your hotel, and even the smallest guesthouses will arrange to send postcards home for you.

While there are still Internet cafés in the region, these days they have been superseded by businesses that offer free Wi-Fi with the expectation that you have a device to take advantage of it. Many restaurants and coffee shops have Wi-Fi, as well as spas and massage parlors. Even if you're staying in an 800 baht-per-night guesthouse, you may find a solid Wi-Fi signal in your guest room.

LAUNDRY SERVICES

There are no real wash-and-dry launderettes on the island, but there are plenty of places to get your laundry done inexpensively. If you are staying in any of the popular beach towns, including Patong, Kamala, Kata, or Karon, there will be plenty of shops offering laundry services, sometimes as a side business to a convenience store or even a coffee shop, so keep an eye out for little signs, and ask if necessary. Nearly every hotel, even cheap bungalows, will have some laundry services, too. Take advantage of this when planning your packing. Expect to pay 50-100 baht per kilogram. Prices will be substantially higher in larger resorts, which often charge by the piece.

LUGGAGE STORAGE

There is luggage storage at the Phuket airport at a rate of 60 baht per day per item; it's to the left just after you exit the baggage-claim area. Many hotels and guesthouses will also store your luggage for a small fee.

Transportation

GETTING THERE

Although Phuket is an island, it is connected to the mainland by a short bridge, making boat travel unnecessary unless you are coming from one of the smaller islands in the region (such as Phi Phi or Lanta). Many people take advantage of the inexpensive flights from Bangkok, but it is also easy to travel overland to the island.

Air

Phuket has one international airport, the Phuket International Airport (tel. 07/632-7230 to 07/632-7237, http://phuketairportthai.com) located in the northwest part of the island on Thep Kasattri Road, serving passengers arriving from all over the world.

If you're coming from Bangkok, it's cheap and easy to get to Phuket by air. Between regular and low-cost airlines, there are more than 20 flights per day, and even during peak travel it is unlikely you won't be able to find a flight on the day you want to leave (although you're better off making reservations in advance if you are traveling in December-January). The low-cost carriers, including Nok Air and Air Asia, often have same-day flights available for less than 2,000 baht each way. Unless it's peak season or Sunday night (when Bangkok residents are returning from weekend getaways), you can literally show up at the airport and ask for the next available flight. Flights are just over an hour from the city, making Phuket an easy place to go even for a weekend.

Flights from Bangkok to Phuket and Krabi are still running from both the new Suvarnabhumi airport and the old airport, Don Muang, which was supposed to be decommissioned after the new airport was built, but was reopened for domestic flights while repair work was being done on the new airport and seems to be lingering. The situation is supposed to be temporary, and the old airport feels makeshift, with very limited food or modern airport comforts. There is only one terminal open, so you won't have to worry about going to the wrong place, but if you're taking a taxi to the airport in Bangkok, make sure the driver understands which one you are going to. Make sure you understand, too. It's not uncommon for carriers to book you on a flight from Don Muang going to Phuket but returning to Suvarnabhumi.

Train

Phuket does not have rail service, but you can take a train to Surat Thani (actually Phun Phin, about 10 minutes by car outside of Surat Thani), and then switch to a bus for the remainder of the journey. An overnight second-class sleeper to Surat Thani will cost around 650 baht, and there are also a couple of trains leaving during the day. The train ride is around 14 hours, then you'll switch to a bus, which you need to pick up in town, although there are cheap buses from the train station to Surat Thani. The bus from Surat Thani to Phuket is about five hours and costs under 200 baht. The whole journey will take around 20 hours, making taking a bus directly from Bangkok a little more appealing (and less expensive).

Bus

There are frequent buses to Phuket from Bangkok and other parts of the country. If you're coming from Bangkok, you can take a bus straight from the Southern Bus Terminal into Phuket. The journey takes around 12 hours and costs 625 baht for the air-conditioned luxury bus run by Phuket Central Tour (tel. 02/434-3233 or 07/621-3615). Other air-conditioned government express buses cost around 500 baht.

If you're heading to Phuket from Bangkok, watch out for tour companies running their own buses, especially those originating in the Khao San Road area. They can be cheaper than government buses and seem more convenient since they leave from the center of the city. But oftentimes you'll arrive at the departure point at the scheduled time only to have to wait another hour or more as other passengers arrive. Government buses leaving from the Southern Bus Terminal are generally prompt, and the air-conditioned buses are surprisingly pleasant. Seats are comfortable and recline, there is a bathroom on board, and

Phuket bus

you'll be given a blanket if you take an overnight bus.

If you're coming from Krabi, there are frequent daily buses to Phuket; the cost is less than 200 baht, and they take about four hours. You can also travel between Phuket and Phang Nga by bus. The ride is about 2.5 hours and it costs under 150 baht.

Car

Depending on where you're coming from, it's easy to drive into Phuket (the island is connected by bridge to Phang Nga), and since getting around once you're there can be expensive, a car could come in handy. Phuket is best reached from Highway 4, which runs north-south down the peninsula. To get to Phuket, you have to travel through Phang Nga Province to get to the Surin Bridge, and the turnoff from the highway is at Route 402, which is well signed in English indicating that it's the route to take to get to Phuket. Route 402 is called Thep Kasattri Road; it runs inland down the island and is where the airport is located.

GETTING AROUND
Taxi

Over the past few years, taxi service on Phuket has become more expensive and less regulated, leading many to refer to Phuket taxi drivers and companies as the "taxi mafia." Metered taxis are generally hard to come by in Phuket, but drivers are supposed to follow a regulated price list for trips between common areas. Expect to pay 400-800 baht to get from the airport to your hotel. The official taxi stand is on the right of the arrivals terminal once you exit the building. Although there will be many people offering you taxis the minute you step out of the terminal, just walk to the taxi stand and take one from there, as it's almost always a better deal.

In every beach village, there are taxi stands for unmetered taxis with prices posted. Expect to pay at least 300 baht for any trip you take with one of these cars. If you're traveling farther than the next beach town, prices will be higher. To get back to the airport from your hotel will generally run around 800 baht if you're in the southern part of the island and slightly less the closer you are to the airport.

Tuk Tuk

The most common way to get around the island is by *tuk tuk*. Not quite like the three-wheeled version seen all over Bangkok and Chiang Mai, the Phuket version is more like a small pickup truck with seats in the back facing backward and forward. They're often painted in bright colors or carry advertisements for local businesses, and some of them also have bright neon lights. You can't miss them—they look like mini disco buses. In Patong, you'll find rows of *tuk tuks* lined up on the main road waiting for customers. When none are waiting, you can just flag one down. It's best to settle on a price before you get into the *tuk tuk,* and generally it's around 200 baht to get to a nearby beach, more for farther destinations. They don't have seat belts—or doors, for that matter—so if you're traveling with small kids, be advised.

Motorcycle Taxi

Motorcycles are less common in Phuket than in Bangkok, but they can be found in very developed areas such as Phuket Town and Patong. Drivers wear brightly colored vests, often with white numbers on the back, and will negotiate fares to take you where you need to go. Prices range anywhere from 50 baht to get from one part of a beach to another to a few hundred baht if you are traveling farther.

Motorcycle Rental

Many people rent motorcycles to get around Phuket. Mostly you'll find 100 cc and 110 cc bikes, which have a clutchless shift system (you still have to change gears with your left foot, but you don't need to squeeze a clutch to do so), but there are also lots of places renting newer scooters that are totally automatic.

At around 250 baht per day (slightly more

in high season or if you're in a remote area), it's the cheapest form of transportation you'll be able to find on the island. It's also a great way to see Phuket, since you're totally mobile and you can come and go as you please. The downside is that some of the roads are windy and hilly, which can be challenging or scary for new riders, and that some parts of Phuket are as congested as large cities. Also, riding a motorcycle anywhere is dangerous. If you rent one, make sure you know what you are doing, and always wear your helmet. You may feel like the only person on the island with one on, but you'll avoid potentially expensive and inconvenient traffic tickets, as the Phuket police occasionally crack down on helmetless riders.

Car Rental

There are numerous international and local car rental companies on the island. While a car isn't necessary, this is a great option if you have children. Although not all of the agencies will require this, it's best to go to an auto club office at home to get an international driver's license before arriving. You can legally drive in Thailand without one, but for insurance reasons some companies will ask that you have it anyway. Brush up on your skills driving a car with a manual transmission before you arrive, as there are few automatic transmission cars available on Phuket.

Avis (arrival terminal, Phuket International Airport, tel. 07/635-1243, www.avisthailand.com, 8am-9pm daily) has a rental counter right at the airport, and you can book online and pick up your car when you arrive.

Andaman Car Rent (51/11 Mu 3, Cherngtalay Rd., Surin Beach, tel. 07/632-4422, www.andamancarrent.com, 9am-9pm daily) is located on Surin Beach and has a good selection of Jeeps and other sport vehicles as well as regular cars. They'll pick you up from the airport if you arrange it ahead of time.

Via Phuket (120/18 Rat-U-Thit Rd., Patong Beach, tel. 07/634-1660, www.viaphuket.com, 8am-5pm Mon.-Sat.) has off-road vehicles in addition to normal cars and will pick you up and drop you off wherever you are staying.

Braun Car Rental (66/29 Soi Veerakit, Nanai Rd., Patong Beach, tel. 07/629-6619, www.braun-rentacar.com, 9am-9pm daily) is on Patong Beach and will do pickup and drop-off at the airport or at your hotel. Braun also rents car seats for a small fee.

Andaman Coast

Highlights

★ **Mu Ko Similan National Park:** This group of small islands offers some of the best diving opportunities in the world (page 67).

★ **Rai Le Beach:** Dramatic limestone cliffs along with warm, clear, emerald-colored water and plenty of outdoor activities make the beach on the west side of Rai Le in Krabi perhaps Thailand's best beach destination (page 71).

★ **Ton Sai Bay:** This is the most popular area of Ko Phi Phi, drawing crowds of day-trippers. The scenery is amazing, as are the diving and snorkeling options surrounding it (page 80).

★ **Khlong Dao Beach:** This beach is beautiful and quiet, and it has just enough amenities and accommodations choices, with none of the overcrowding found at some of the more popular island destinations (page 87).

★ **Ko Kradan:** Arguably the prettiest island in Trang, Ko Kradan offers amazing views of neighboring islands and accessible reefs for snorkelers (page 94).

If paradise were a place on earth, it would be somewhere on the Andaman coast of Thailand. The region is astoundingly beautiful—bright, clear, warm water teeming with wildlife from tropical fish to magnificent coral, even occasional sea cows and reef sharks (the kind that don't eat people). The coast and islands have sandy beaches, and there are hundreds of small islands and limestone rock formations rising up out of the ocean. Inland, there are tropical rainforests, mangrove swamps, mountains, and waterfalls. If it's an active vacation you're looking for, there are abundant opportunities to snorkel, dive, sea kayak, or hike, especially in the numerous national parks.

But it's not just the physical beauty and activities that make the area such a great traveling experience. The region still offers a chance to glimpse rural and small-city life in Thailand. While Phuket has attracted residents from all over the world as well as transplants from Bangkok and other parts of the country, and largely feels like a commercialized tourist destination, if you travel north to Phang Nga Province, you'll find small fishing villages along the coast where fishing families can often be found clearing nets at the end of the day or setting out squid to dry in the sun. To the south, in Satun, you'll find a largely Muslim population and a fascinating blend of Islam and Buddhism evidenced in the houses of worship and the dress of the local people.

In the past few decades, Phuket has really blossomed into a world-class destination for vacationers from all over the world, with all of the pros and cons that go with it. But traveling either north to Phang Nga or south to Krabi and Trang, things slow down again, although even in Trang there are more and more bungalows, resorts, and hotels for visitors being built every year. Though many travelers go to one spot on the Andaman and plant themselves there for the duration, if you want to both indulge and explore, it's an easy place to be a little more adventurous. Public and private buses can take you from Phuket or Krabi either north or south along the coast, and if you rent a car, you'll find the highway system

---

The Andaman Coast

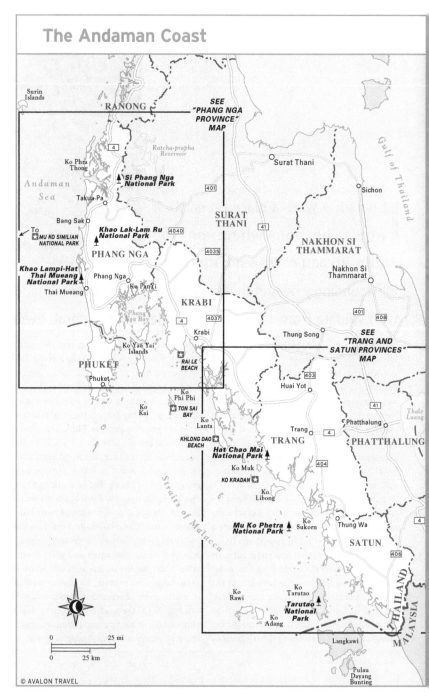

Surin Islands

RANONG

SEE "PHANG NGA PROVINCE" MAP

4

Ratcha-prapha Reservoir

Ko Phra Thong

Si Phang Nga National Park

Surat Thani

Sichon

Andaman Sea

Takua Pa

401

Bang Sak

SURAT THANI

41

To MU KO SIMILIAN NATIONAL PARK

Khao Lak-Lam Ru National Park

4040

NAKHON SI THAMMARAT

PHANG NGA

4035

Khao Lampi-Hat Thai Mueang National Park

Phang Nga

Nakhon Si Thammarat

Ko Panyi

Thai Mueang

KRABI

401

408

Phang Nga Bay

4

4037

Thung Song

SEE "TRANG AND SATUN PROVINCES" MAP

Krabi

Ko Yao Yai Islands

PHUKET

RAI LE BEACH

Phuket

403

Huai Yot

Ko Phi Phi

41

Thale Luang

Ko Kai

TON SAI BAY

Ko Lanta

Phatthalung

KHLONG DAO BEACH

Hat Chao Mai National Park

Trang

TRANG

4

PHATTHALUNG

Ko Muk

404

KO KRADAN

Ko Libong

Mu Ko Phetra National Park

Ko Sukorn

Thung Wa

4

SATUN

406

Straits of Malacca

Gulf of Thailand

Ko Rawi

Ko Tarutao

Tarutao National Park

THAILAND

Ko Adang

MALAYSIA

0   25 mi

0   25 km

Langkawi

M

Pulau Dayang Bunting

exceptionally well maintained and generally navigable, even if you can't read a word of Thai.

The Andaman coast is also perfect for island-hopping, and the best way to do that is by boat. There are plenty of ferries, speedboats, and longtails to take you from island to island and beach to beach. You can fly into Phuket, spend a few days on one of the nearby beaches, then take a boat to Phi Phi, Ko Lanta, or one of the other numerous islands in Phang Nga Bay, or hit 3-4 islands in one trip; there are hundreds of islands in the region to choose from. Some, such as Phi Phi, are arguably overpopulated with travelers and resorts. But there are still some beautiful islands you can stay on that feel less exploited by tourism and kinder to the natural surroundings.

Prices are still amazingly reasonable considering the physical landscape. Even in the most coveted areas, you'll be able to find simple accommodations, sometimes right on the beach, for less than US$40 per night, even cheaper the farther away from Phuket you are. Of course, if you're looking for five-star luxury, you'll be able to find that, too. Some of the best resorts in the world have Andaman coast addresses.

PLANNING YOUR TIME

How you plan your time depends mostly on what you want to get out of your vacation. If you're hoping to pick a beach on the Andaman coast, grab a chair, and sit and relax for the duration of your time in Thailand, you won't need to do much planning at all.

If you do choose to explore some of the region's surrounding islands, remember that getting from one place to another can often take a few hours and involve taking land transportation to a pier and then a sometimes-long boat ride, especially if you are relying on public transportation. Many tour operators offer day trips to surrounding islands from Krabi or Phuket, and these can be an excellent way to see many different places at once, although you won't have any control over the schedule or itinerary.

If you really want to explore each island (or stay overnight), your best bet is to take one of the large ferries from Phuket to Ko Phi Phi, Ko Lanta, or Krabi and then use the smaller longtail boats to take you to other islands in the vicinity. Some people prefer to base themselves on one of the more built-up islands (Ko Lanta or Ko Phi Phi) and explore the surrounding islands on day trips, but it's just as easy to sleep on different islands or even camp at one of the island national parks. If you plan on island-hopping, make sure to pack light. Longtail boats, which are colorful wooden boats used for short trips, are small, usually not covered, and sometimes a little leaky. There's no room for a large suitcase or even a very large backpack. It is also possible to charter a sailboat or speedboat to island-hop, but the cost is in the thousands of dollars for a multiday trip.

If you've come to the region primarily to dive, you'll actually find it much easier to get around, as there are numerous large dive boats offering live-aboard, multiday dive trips that will take you to some of the best diving sites in the country. Trips generally depart from Phuket, Krabi, and Khao Lak.

Phang Nga Province, north of Phuket on the mainland, is home to the spectacular Phang Nga Bay, which overlaps with Phuket and Krabi. But aside from this well-known tourist spot, traveling north along the west coast, the region has beautiful beaches and a mountainous, forested interior. It's also home to the Surin and Similan National Marine Parks off the coast. With plentiful coral, this is some of the best diving and snorkeling in the country. The mainland beaches are arguably as top-notch as those in Phuket and Krabi, and the area is more visited by travelers every year. Although there are world-class resorts, and the lower part of the region is easily reached from the Phuket airport (to Khao Lak it's about the same drive as to parts of southern Phuket), it's definitely quieter. There's nothing even close to the density of Phuket's Patong Beach, so it is perfect for those looking for a slightly off-the-beaten-track experience without having to cut out any amenities.

PHANG NGA BAY

Surrounded by Phuket to the west, Phang Nga Province to the north, and Krabi to the east, Phang Nga Bay is filled with small islands and rock formations rising out of the sea, creating breathtaking scenery that, for many, is what the Andaman coast is all about. There are more than 100 islands in the bay; some, such as Ko Yao Noi, are large enough for accommodations, and some, such as "James Bond Island," are so small that they're barely more than rocks. In addition to some sandy beaches, the bay's islands and surrounding coasts are also home to verdant mangrove swamps. You may be able to sight egrets, kingfishers, and herons. There are hidden lagoons inside some of the islands where you can snorkel or swim in sheltered waters, and caves on some of the islands from the continued erosion of the limestone material they're primarily made of. The relatively shallow waters create amazing ocean colors, from light blue when the sun is shining to deep emerald, and despite the fact that you'll probably be plying the waters and exploring the caves with thousands of visitors from all over the world, it's worth the crowds and the slightly commercialized feeling of the area just to enjoy the physical landscape.

There is only one public ferry to the bay, traveling from the east side of Phuket to Ko Yao Noi. To tour the bay, you'll either need to arrange a group tour with one of the many travel agents in the region or hire a private boat from Phang Nga. There are many agencies offering tours, and it can be a convenient way to see the area.

Islands

Ko Pan Yi (เกาะปันหยี, Sea Gypsy Island) is really a large cluster of houses, shops, and even a mosque built on stilts right over the water next to a small rocky island, a sort of Water World-esque village in the middle of the sea. The people living in the village are primarily Muslim fisherfolk, who used to make their living plying the surrounding waters but now have seen much of their existence subsidized by the thousands of tourists who visit each day and who buy food and drinks on the island. The island is quite picturesque, but it's not inhabited by the traditional sea gypsies of the region, called Moken, a nomadic people who spend months at a time at sea.

About one hour by boat from Krabi, the **Mu Ko Hong Islands** (หมู่เกาะห้อง) are made up of stunning limestone formations surrounded by coral reefs with some sandy beaches. Although the islands are too small to have any accommodations, they can be visited during day trips and for snorkeling, canoeing, or kayaking. One of the larger islands in the group, Ko Hong, has a small hiking trail.

The islands of **Ko Yao** (เกาะยาว) are the largest in Phang Nga Bay and comprise the

Phang Nga Province

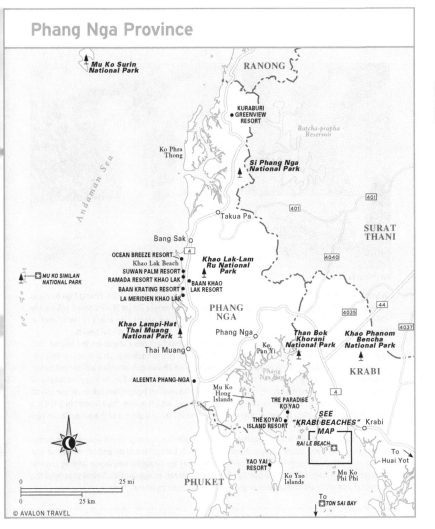

© AVALON TRAVEL

larger **Ko Yao Yai** and the smaller **Ko Yao Noi** to the north. Just a couple of hours by ferry from the mainland, the Ko Yao islands are amazingly untouched by the rampant tourism that seems to have changed even the smallest islands from places supported by local industry and quiet refuges for indigenous animals to bungalow- and bar-laden resort spots. Here it's dirt roads, water buffalo, and dense green forest. Perhaps this is because the beaches are not as beautiful as

some of the others in the area—at low tide it's just too rocky to swim. Still, if you are looking to get away somewhere quiet and feel like you're actually in Thailand, these islands provide a truly special experience. The local culture is primarily Muslim Thai, and there's much less of a party scene; it can even be hard to find a beer at the handful of small restaurants. Both islands have accommodations, even a couple of luxury resorts, although the smaller Ko Yao Noi has the most options for

James Bond Island

Ko Phing Kan

When the James Bond thriller *The Man with the Golden Gun* came out in 1974, Phang Nga Bay was barely known by anyone outside Thailand. The tiny island where Roger Moore stood is formally called Ko Phing Kan, but it's often referred to as James Bond Island. Like many of the islands in Phang Nga Bay, it has spectacular karst topography and a small but beautiful beach.

Fast-forward three decades, and little Ko Phing Kan has become a staple on the tourist trail. During high season, literally hundreds of people visit the island each day, a trip that's often combined with a visit to Ko Pan Yi to see the "sea gypsies" of Thailand. Instead of a deserted beach in paradise, as seen in the film, the beach is now crammed full of vendors selling postcards and other tourist items. And everyone, it seems, wants to have his or her picture taken on the island, against a backdrop of the spectacular Ko Tapu. Ko Tapu, which means "nail island" in Thai, is a beautiful karst formation towering about 180 meters (591 ft) straight out of the water; it can also be seen in the film.

Many tour companies will encourage visitors to take this day trip, and if you're a big James Bond movie buff, you might enjoy it despite the crowds being herded on and off the island. But bear in mind that although the islands of Phang Nga Bay are beautiful and worth visiting, marine ecosystems are fragile. There are plenty of stunning islands to see, and it's better to spread the impact of our visits around instead of piling it all onto one tiny island.

places to stay. So far, there are no ATMs on the island (although this may be changing soon), so bring plenty of cash from the mainland if you're planning on hanging out here. To get to Ko Yao, you can take a longtail boat from the Bang Rong pier on the east coast of Phuket. There are daily ferries at 9:30am, noon, and 5pm.

Sea Kayaking
Phang Nga Bay is a great kayaking destination. You can explore the smaller islands that have lagoons, caves, and no beaches to land on. Many kayaking trips originate from Phuket, where you can make arrangements for a daylong or multiple-day trip to the area.

Accommodations and Food
If you want to stay on Ko Yao but are looking for something in the budget category, the **Yao Yai Resort** (Mu 7, Ban Lopareh,

tel. 08/5784-3043, www.yaoyairesort.com, 1,000B) has some very cheap little wooden bungalows with their own small outdoor sitting areas. The guest rooms are not spectacular, but they are clean, and many of them have air-conditioning. There's no pool, but there is a small restaurant on the premises and a nice beach.

The Paradise Ko Yao (24 Mu 4, Ko Yao Noi, tel. 07/623-8081 or 08/1892-4878, www.theparadise.biz, 7,500B) is a contemporary but casual bungalow resort with very well-designed, open, airy guest rooms, many with their own sitting rooms that open to the surrounding landscape of Phang Nga Bay. Some of the guest rooms even have whirlpool tubs. The grounds are set in the hills, which are speckled with the thatched roofs of the bungalows, and they also have a very chic infinity swimming pool.

This is the place to go if you want to experience that secluded desert-island feeling with a little luxury. The Koyao Island Resort (24/2 Mu 5, Ko Yao Noi, tel. 07/659-7474 to 07/659-7476, www.koyao.com, 8,000B) has some beautiful villas set right on the beach, each with a charming rustic feeling but without compromising on amenities such as air-conditioning or nice baths. There's also a small spa and a beautiful swimming pool.

Few properties in the world, let alone in Thailand, can compete with the reputation the Six Senses Yao Noi (56 Mu 5, Ko Yao Noi, www.sixsenses.com, 15,000B) has built up over the years. The sprawling property offers only private villas, and each is located far enough away from the rest to feel totally secluded. The understated decor, with mostly natural materials, allows the amazing views and natural surroundings to take center stage. Service is impeccable, and many who stay here say they have never been better cared for. Although Ko Yao Noi is not a private island, the resort feels very much like a secret hideaway of the rich and famous; perhaps it helps that you can arrive by private seaplane or helicopter if you choose.

Since most of these islands are visited as day trips, the only food you'll find is very casual beach dining. Ko Pan Yi, a popular lunch stop for boat tours, has some reasonable restaurants right on the water, serving seafood and other Thai dishes, and Ko Yao has some similar spots to eat.

If you're staying at one of the resorts, meals are not included, but each of the accommodations listed has a reasonable restaurant on-site.

Transportation

As Phang Nga Bay is bordered by Phuket, Krabi, Phang Nga, and Trang to the south, there are a number of different launching points from which to see the islands. If you are flying into Phuket airport, it's actually easier to get a boat from Phuket than to drive to Phang Nga and seek sea transportation from there. Phuket is so heavily visited that many of the tours around Phang Nga Bay will originate at one of the Phuket marinas. Krabi is also a very popular launch point, and if you fly into Krabi, you'll most likely be taking a boat from Ao Nang.

If you are staying at one of the island resorts, they will advise you of the best way to get there (the nicer ones will arrange transportation for you). If you're going for a day trip, you'll most likely do it as part of an organized tour leaving from Phuket or Krabi; these tours almost always pick you up from your hotel and bring you back in the evening. Tours advertising trips to Ko Pan Yi or "James Bond Island" are good for viewing the bay, and if they don't include snorkeling or other activities, they will cost around 500 baht per person. Many of the small islands don't have consistent ferry service, so if you want to spend the day on one of them without a tour, you will have to hire a boat to take you out. You can hire a boat from Phuket marina, but you'll probably pay hundreds of dollars, since the only boats that can access the bay from there are speedboats. If you're coming from Phang Nga, you'll be able to hire a private boat for a couple of hours from the Ao Phang Nga National Park visitors center in Tha Dan.

Expect to pay around 1,000 baht for two hours.

If you're driving, the only island in the bay you'll be able to access is Ko Lanta. Otherwise, plan on driving to Tha Dan, Krabi, or Phuket and leaving your car there to switch to sea transportation.

KHAO LAMPI-HAT THAI MUANG NATIONAL PARK
อุทยานแห่งชาติเขาลำ
ปี –หาดท้ายเหมือง

The Khao Lampi-Hat Thai Muang National Park (Mu 5, Amphoe Thai Muang, Phang Nga, tel. 08/4059-7879 or 07/641-7206, 8:30am-6pm daily, 400B) is a small national park on just over 7,200 hectares of land and water that is best known for some spectacular waterfalls, including the Namtok Lampi, a three-tiered waterfall that runs all year. The waterfall is about 13 kilometers (8 mi) from the park headquarters on the beach; to get there you'll need to drive most of the way along the main road (there are plenty of signs for the waterfall) and then take a short walk to the falls.

Another great waterfall to explore is Namtok Ton Phrai, the largest in the park (although like most waterfalls in the country, it will be less impressive during dry season). These falls are about 11 kilometers (7 mi) from the park's headquarters on the beach, and there are marked roads from there. There is also a ranger station here and a canteen, as it is one of the most popular spots in the park. If you're looking for a quiet beach, Hat Thai Muang is a 13-kilometer (8 mi) stretch of sandy beach with clear blue waters. If you visit November-February, you may see sea turtles coming to lay their eggs on shore at night, and park rangers collecting the eggs to incubate them safe from poachers or predators in their nursery (this is the main reason the beach is a protected national park). In March there's a festival in which locals and visitors watch the little baby turtles make their way to the sea after hatching.

The park has both bungalows for rent and camping areas where you can pitch a tent. There are some small food vendors around during the day in addition to the canteen at Namtok Lampi.

Transportation
By car from Phuket airport or anywhere on Highway 4, head straight north to Phang Nga on Highway 4 for about 56 kilometers (35 mi) to the Tai Muang Market, where you'll see a sign for the national park. Turn off the main road onto Route 401 for about 6.5 kilometers (4 mi).

There are frequent buses from Bangkok to Phang Nga, which often traverse the popular Highway 4 and terminate in Phuket; they cost 400-500 baht for an air-conditioned bus. From Phang Nga to the park, you can pick up a normal local bus for about 30 baht or an air-conditioned bus for 45 baht.

KHAO LAK
ตะกั่วป่า

Just an hour's drive from the Phuket airport is Takua Pa Province, although it's often referred to as Khao Lak (the name of a part of the province). Despite being literally washed away by the 2004 tsunami, the area is once again an up-and-coming resort area with beautiful beaches, scenic mountain ranges with rainforest in the background, and some luxurious resorts and quaint bungalows. Although more travelers are visiting the area every year, especially in Khao Lak, and you'll see some big brand-name accommodations, it still feels much quieter and more relaxed than any beach you'll find on Phuket.

Khao Lak-Lam Ru National Park
อุทยานแห่งชาติเขาหลัก–ลำรู่

Spanning four provinces, the Khao Lak-Lam Ru National Park (Mu 7, Khuk Khak, Takua Pa, tel. 07/648-5243, 8:30am-6pm daily, 400B), named after the large mountain within its borders, Khao Lak, has kilometers of pristine beach and thick forest. There are a number of small waterfalls, including the Lam Ru waterfall, a five-tiered waterfall hidden amid thick trees. During the day the park is populated not only with visitors but also with beautiful butterflies and exotic birds. If you feel like camping, there is a campground with some limited facilities and just a few bungalows available for rent. Khao Lak Beach is also part of the park, and although parts of the beach are too rocky for swimming, there are some sandy patches where you can lay out a towel and enjoy the view of the Andaman Sea.

Beaches and Islands

The Khao Lak Beach region, close to the bridge connecting Phuket with the mainland, offers clean, quiet stretches of beach with amazing crystal-clear waters. From north to south, there are three beaches: Bang Niang, Nang Thong, and Sunset. Together they take up about eight kilometers (5 mi) of coastline. Khao Lak has traditionally been a hangout for divers, since it's an easy place to set off to the Similan or Surin Islands, and thus remains a laid-back, rustic place to visit. There are lots of dive shops, a handful of restaurants, and the Andaman Sea to keep you occupied.

About 32 kilometers (20 mi) north of Khao Lak is Bang Sak, even less developed than its neighbor to the north, which has attracted some luxury resorts in the past few years. There's no nightlife in the area, but if you're looking for a place to be based for some diving or looking to enjoy the water and the convenience of the Phuket airport without dealing with crowds, this is a great spot. The beach is really spectacular: The shore is wide and flat, and the white sands are smooth and relatively unmarred by rocks.

Diving and Snorkeling

Divers in Khao Lak will be able to get to many of the places listed in the Phuket chapter. The waters surrounding the Andaman coast and its islands offer diverse marinelife and dive sites from beginner to advanced, some considered among the best in the world. The biggest draws for trips out of Khao Lak are the Similan Islands and the Surin Islands, as they are farther north and therefore easier to get to from Khao Lak. However, you can still get trips from Phuket and Phuket dive shops will also drive guests from Phuket to Khao Lak and then put them onto boats there. Most dive shops offer dives to all of the most popular sites in the region.

Diving is really Khao Lak's reason for being a tourist destination, so it's no surprise that there are so many diving shops in the area. The following outfitters are PADI certified. Check the PADI website (www.padi.com) for more.

- Wicked Diving (4/17 Mu 7, Khao Lak, tel. 07/648-5868, www.wickeddiving.com)
- Khao Lak Explorer (13/43 Mu 7, Petchkasem Rd., Khao Lak, tel. 07/648-5308, www.khaolakexplorer.com)
- Liquid Liveboards (13/43 Mu 7, Khao Lak, tel. 07/648-5069, www.liquid-adventure.com)
- Sea Dragon Dive Center (5/51 Mu 7, Petchkasem Rd., Khao Lak, tel. 07/648-5420, www.seadragondivecenter.com)

Accommodations

Ocean Breeze Resort (26/3 Mu 7, Khuk Khak, Takua Pa, www.gerdnoi.com, tel. 07/648-5145, 1,800B), formerly called Gerd & Noi Bungalows, isn't very fancy, but it is located right on the beach and has clean, very family-friendly accommodations. The larger bungalows can easily sleep a small family, and there's a small swimming pool and a restaurant serving Thai and European food. The vibe is like old Khao Lak—laid-back and unpretentious.

If you plan to spend some time doing a liveaboard diving trip to the outer islands, the Kuraburi Greenview Resort (140/89 Mu 3, Kura, Kuraburi, tel. 07/640-1400, www.kuraburigreenviewresort.com, 1,900B) has some charming cabins in which to base yourself at superbudget prices. The cabins and guest rooms look like they would be more appropriate in New England than Southeast Asia, with lots of exposed wood and rocks along

64

with views of the grounds. The hotel runs lots of dive and snorkeling trips and can arrange live-aboards on their boats, but the hotel itself is not right on the water.

Just south of Bang Sak, Baan Khao Lak Resort (26/16 Mu 7, Petchkasem Rd., Khuk Khak, Takua Pa, tel. 07/648-5198, www.baankhaolak.com, 3,500B) is a great value, even during the high season. All of the guest rooms and villas are modern, stylish, and well maintained, and the grounds of this resort on the beach are lushly landscaped and have lots of amenities you wouldn't expect for the price, including a pool right on the beach, restaurants, and an outdoor beach bar. This is a family-friendly property and also one of the rare resorts in the country that have wheelchair-accessible rooms and grounds.

Set on Bang Niang, La Flora Resort and Spa (59/1 Mu 5, Khuk Khak Rd., Takua Pa, tel. 07/642-8000, 5,500B) is a surprisingly large resort, with over 100 guest rooms and villas set on a quiet stretch of beach. The guest rooms are spacious and designed with a modern Thai theme, and the best are the villas on the beach. While the area may be quiet, the resort's restaurants, spa, gorgeous swimming pool, and even free Wi-Fi will keep you occupied.

For a smaller resort experience, Baan Krating Resort (28 Mu 7, Khuk Khak, Takua Pa, tel. 07/648-5188 or 07/648-5189, www.baankrating.com, 2,000B), next to Khao Lak-Lam Ru National Park, has rustic grounds set in the cliffs overlooking the ocean and peppered with wooden bungalows connected via walkway. Each of the guest rooms is individually decorated, but you won't have to do without nice sheets and decent baths if you decide to stay here, as the bungalows, although not brand new, are definitely not in the budget category. The pool and common areas are small, as is the resort, but there's a restaurant on the premises, and the view of Khao Lak Bay is amazing. This is definitely a place for the young and agile: Depending on where your bungalow is, you may be climbing stairs.

The Suwan Palm Resort (30/27 Mu 7, Khuk Khak, Takua Pa, tel. 07/648-5830, www.suwanpalm.com, 3,000B) is on the same beach as some of Khao Lak's most expensive properties, and although it's not a luxury chain, it does offer guests clean, modern guest rooms, a nice swimming pool, a bar and restaurant on the premises, and even a small spa. The facilities are small but sufficient for those whose primary goal is to enjoy the beach. Low-season rates can be an excellent value.

The Ramada Resort Khao Lak (59 Mu 5, Khuk Khak, Takua Pa, tel. 07/642-7777, www.ramadakhaolak.com, 3,500B), though not quite as nice as Le Meridien, is a nice new resort set on a beautiful strip of beach. The guest rooms are large and modern, and some have unobstructed views of the Andaman Sea. Pool villas are compact but a great value for those who want some privacy. The property's main swimming pool, which is just behind the beach, is massive. There is also a spa, a fitness center, and an activity program for kids.

The JW Marriott Khao Lak (41/12 Mu 3, Khuk Khak, Khao Lak, tel. 081/270-9760, www.marriott.com, 4,000B) is a gorgeous, massive luxury resort with expansive grounds and a prime location right on the beach. Rooms are large, modern, and tastefully decorated with regional art and textiles. The central swimming pool is enormous. Additional facilities include a fitness center, full-service spa, and a kids' club. You definitely will not want for anything at this resort, and though it isn't cheap by any means, it's a good value considering what you get for your money. There is a good variety of food and drink on the premises, or you can walk out for local food. This resort is very popular with families and has good facilities and rooms for small children.

★ Le Meridien Khao Lak (9/9 Mu 1, Khuk Khak, Takua Pa, tel. 07/642-7500, www.starwoodhotels.com, 5,000B) is one of the nicest resorts in the area. The nine-hectare grounds are lush and well manicured, with a large child-friendly pool and direct beach access. The guest rooms are modern, airy, and comfortable, with dark-wood details and crisp linens. The villas are spacious, although they can cost significantly more than the rooms. There's a beautiful spa on the premises and a charming Thai restaurant. Although this is a large chain resort, there's no generic feeling here.

The small, luxurious Sarojin (60 Mu 2, Khuk Khak, Takua Pa, tel. 07/648-5830, www.sarojin.com, 7,000B) resort, located right on the beach, has large, comfortable guest rooms and suites filled with modern Thai-style furnishings. The grounds are lush and spacious and include shaded *salas* (pavilions) for lounging at the large modern pool as well as a high-end spa. The resort's restaurant and bar options are a little pricey, but the breakfast, included in most rates, has lots of variety and is served 'til late. Service in general is excellent and attentive, and this is a great choice for a romantic getaway or honeymoon.

Casa de La Flora (67/213 Mu 5, Khuk Khak, Takua Pa, tel. 07/642-8999, www.casadelaflora.com, 7,000B), not to be confused with the larger, less expensive La Flora Resort and Spa, is a modern, minimalist, high-end, small boutique resort on the beach. All accommodations are suites or villas, and most have fantastic views of the beach. The architecture, simple materials, and very basic shapes are striking. Stand-alone villas are basic concrete boxes with ample windows to allow in plenty of natural light. There is also a large, beautiful swimming pool on the grounds, as well as a spa, fitness center, and restaurant.

Just south of the Khao Lak area, and only a few kilometers from the Sarasin Bridge to Phuket, is the ★ Aleenta Phang-Nga (33 Mu 5, Khok Kloi, Takua Pa, tel. 02/508-5333, www.aleenta.com, 12,000B), at the top of the class of small boutique resorts in Thailand. The villas are swanky and contemporary, with a blend of Mediterranean and Thai styling; some are full apartments with living areas and small private pools. The common areas are small, but the restaurant has an excellent East-West menu. Little touches, including iPods in every guest room and scented oil burners, will make you feel pampered. This is definitely a place you're likely to find incognito movie stars.

Food

For a little bit of everything, and cocktails, too, head to the superpopular Smile Khaolak Restaurant (5/15 Mu 3, Petchkasem Rd., tel. 083/391-2600, 11am-10pm daily, 200B). The menu features mostly standard Thai dishes, including basics such as spring rolls and curries, but it also has an extensive vegetarian menu. The setting is casual but pretty—lots of bamboo and Thai art fill the dining room. Smile is more than a few steps above a shophouse restaurant; make sure to call for reservations. The restaurant is filled with mostly foreign tourists, not a particularly authentic place but a good choice nonetheless.

For straightforward Thai food, head to Everyday Lazy House (89 Mu 3, Petchkasem Rd. at Bang Niang Market, tel. 081/397-2802, 4pm-11pm daily, 300B). The menu features lots of fresh seafood, and also traditional Thai favorites and some very yummy desserts. There is live music many nights, and of course lots of cold beer. This is another very popular restaurant with tourists. There are also cooking classes taught by the staff; call ahead to arrange one.

Hill Tribe Restaurant (13/22 Mu 6, Petchkasem Rd., Khao Lak, tel. 086/283-0933, 1pm-10pm daily, 200B) isn't entirely authentic northern Thai food, but it is a lot more interesting than the basic, tourist-friendly Thai food you'll find at resorts and guesthouses all over the region. Dishes such as banana flower salad and baked duck are worth trying; they also offer a *khan toke* meal, which is essentially a set meal served on a single tray featuring sticky rice and Burmese curry. The dining room here is very casual—triangle pillows, mats, and low tables so you can sit on the floor and eat, though you can choose to sit at a conventional table, too.

Enzo, Bistro Fusion Japanese (62/2 Mu 5, Khuk Khak, Khao Lak, tel. 07/648-6671, 1pm-11pm daily during high season, opens at

3pm during low season, 600B) specializes in fresh sushi and sashimi but also offers other Japanese items, such as tempura and grilled fish and meat. There is a very popular sushi buffet on many evenings during high season. The restaurant is comfortable and homey, and there is nice outdoor seating, too.

Every town needs at least one English pub, and in Khao Lak that's Mars Bar (19/12 Mu 6, Khuk Khak, Khao Lak, tel. 084/746-5951, 8am-11pm daily, 200B). Quiz nights, beer, chips, and kidney pies are all to be found here. The dining room itself isn't much more than a typical Thai shophouse, and the vibe here is very friendly and unpretentious.

The pizza at La Piccola Maria Pizzeria (30/27 Mu 7, Petchkasem Rd., Khao Lak, tel. 087/803-3919, 8am-9pm daily, 250B) isn't going to blow you away, but considering that you are in the middle of a tropical beach area in Asia, these guys do a credible job. They also serve pasta, salad, and some grilled meat, and all food is available for takeout. The little corner restaurant can get very crowded, though with indoor and outdoor seating it can accommodate dozens of people at once.

Transportation

The easiest way to get to Phang Nga is to fly into Phuket International Airport (tel. 07/632-7230 to 07/632-7237, www.phuket-airportthai.com). Since the airport is in the northern part of the island, it's less than an hour's drive from the Sarasin Bridge to Phang Nga. Metered taxis from the airport will drive you to Phang Nga for 300-1,000 baht, depending on where you're going. If you're heading for Khao Lak, expect to pay around 700 baht.

If you're driving, Phang Nga is best reached by car by driving along Highway 4 until you reach Phang Nga, which will be well signed in English.

Buses running from Bangkok to Phuket will always stop in Phang Nga along the way as long as you let the driver know that's where you're going (since Phang Nga is the only land crossing to the island).

KO PHRA THONG
เกาะพระทอง

Separated from the mainland by a channel, mudflats, and mangroves, this little island, just 90 square kilometers (35 sq mi), is named Phra Thong, or golden Buddha, based on a legend that shipwrecked pirates buried a gold statue of the Buddha somewhere on the island. These days, there are no pirates around, and the treasure has never been found, but the island is home to a handful of fishing villages and just a couple of ecofriendly resorts. The beaches on the west side of the island are beautiful, serene, and relatively untouched by commercialism. In addition to the mangroves, sea grass, and patches of rainforest, the island is home to macaques, otters, and lemurs, to name just a few of the small animals you might run into. It's also home to sea turtles that come to bury their eggs on the shore every year. Although the island and neighboring Ko Ra together form one of the newest national parks in the country, there are no national park amenities.

Sports and Recreation

There are plentiful opportunities to hike and walk the island, although there are no established marked trails. If you are staying on the island, the resort will provide you with a map of the areas you can safely explore.

Accommodations

The Golden Buddha Resort (131 Mu 2, Ko Phra Thong, tel. 08/7055-4099, www.goldenbuddharesort.com, 3,500B) is a small, quiet, ecofriendly resort on the west coast of the island. Here you'll find beach yoga and wooden bungalows close to the water, without the typical crowds or prices. You have to forgo luxuries such as air-conditioning and reliable Internet access, but if you're looking for a quiet, remote place on the shore, this is a beautiful spot to relax and unwind. There are also larger houses available for groups.

You can also camp on the island, as it's a national park, although right now there are no bungalows, tent rentals, or canteens, so you have to bring everything you need with you, including water.

Food

There's really no tourism infrastructure set up on the island, so finding food is challenging. If you're staying at the island's resort, they'll make sure to feed you. Otherwise, you may be able to find someone to prepare a meal for you in the villages, slightly inland. If you're coming for the day or camping, pack food and water.

Transportation

To get to Ko Phra Thong, you'll first have to find your way to the Kuraburi pier. If you're driving, take Highway 4 to the Kuraburi district, which is south of Ranong Province and north of Takua Pa and Si Phang Nga National Park. From the pier in Kuraburi, there are no scheduled boats. You can either negotiate with a longtail captain to take you, or if you are staying at the Golden Buddha Resort, they will arrange to have someone pick you up. Expect to pay 1,000-1,500 baht each way, even if you arrange it through the hotel.

★ MU KO SIMILAN NATIONAL PARK

The Similan Islands are a group of nine islands located about 50 miles off the coast of Thailand, west of Khao Lak. They are considered to have the best diving in all of Thailand and some of the best in the world. Here you'll find plenty of colorful reefs and plankton blooms (during the hot season) attracting sharks, rays, and tropical fish. Other parts of the island grouping are more rugged, with boulder formations offering more adventurous diving. There are also great night-diving spots where you'll see squid, crustaceans, and other creatures. These islands can be visited on day trips from Phuket and Khao Lak, but many people choose multiday live-aboards.

Because the Similan Islands are part of a national marine park, Mu Ko Similan National Park (tel. 07/645-3272), and are far from the mainland, access to them is restricted. Depending on the time of year you visit, you will be able to visit some of the islands, but not all, and you'll have to visit them as part of an organized diving or day tour. Though it is frustrating not to have free access to these islands, it is probably for the better, as they (and the coral that has made them so popular) are already starting to show signs of wear and tear from the hundreds of tourists who visit each week.

Beaches and Islands

As islands go, the Similans initially seem less stunning than some of the islands in Phang Nga Bay, with their dramatic limestone formations and beautiful surrounding waters. The Similans are covered in foliage and boulders and are completely uninhabited. But those islands that do have sandy beaches (some do not) have gorgeous light sand thanks to the abundant coral reefs in the area. And once you go below the surface of the water, you'll discover not only coral reefs but underwater rock formations that attract an astounding diversity of marinelife.

The largest and most popular of the islands in this archipelago is Ko Similan. It and Ko Miang are the only two islands visitors are allowed to land on. Both are run by the National Parks of Thailand, which provides very limited accommodations and food service on each.

However you plan your trip, the islands are only open for visitors between November and May; they close completely during the rainy season.

Day Trips

Many of the diving companies listed in Phuket and Khao Lak offer day trips for either diving or snorkeling. It's a long day, as the trip is either 3 hours on a ferryboat or 90 minutes by speedboat, but if you only have a day and want to see this amazing area, it's a great opportunity. Four companies that offer day trips are Wicked Diving (4/17 Mu 7, Khao Lak, tel. 07/648-5868, www.wickeddiving.com), Khao

Lak Explorer (13/43 Mu 7, Petchkasem Rd., Khao Lak, tel. 07/648-5308, www.khaolakexplorer.com), Liquid Liveboards (13/43 Mu 7, Khao Lak, tel. 07/648-5069, www.liquid-adventure.com), and Sea Dragon Dive Center (5/51 Mu 7, Petchkasem Rd., Khao Lak, tel. 07/648-5420, www.seadragondivecenter.com). Trips generally include transfer from your hotel or guesthouse, breakfast, boat to the Similans, and diving or snorkeling equipment. Rates start at 2,500 baht for snorkeling or 4,800 baht for diving, plus national park fees (700B pp).

Overnight Trips and Camping

The only way to stay overnight on Ko Similan or Ko Miang is to stay at one of the park's bungalows or campsites. These are basic bungalows and cabins with running water and electricity. Costs are between 1,000 and 2,000 baht per night, per room. Book accommodations with the Department of National Parks (tel. 02/562-0760, np_income@dnp. go.th). Once the reservation is booked, you must transfer full payment to the National Parks by bank wire (or at a Krung Thai Bank or ATM in Thailand).

Tour companies that offer overnight trips to the islands will make arrangements in advance for you. Even if you do make your own arrangements, there is no ferry between these islands and the mainland or Phuket, so you must contact a tour company for transportation.

Live-Aboards

The most common way to see the Similan Islands, and the world below them, is on a live-aboard boat, where you'll dive during the day and eat, sleep, and hang out on the boat the rest of the time. The quality and size of live-aboards vary tremendously from tour company to tour company (and the type of boat a tour company uses is not necessarily indicative of the quality of dive instruction or supervision you will get). Nearly all of the dive companies listed in Phuket and Khao Lak do live-aboard trips to the Similan Islands. Four

companies that offer live-aboard trips are Wicked Diving (4/17 Mu 7, Khao Lak, tel. 07/648-5868, www.wickeddiving.com), Khao Lak Explorer (13/43 Mu 7, Petchkasem Rd., Khao Lak, tel. 07/648-5308, www.khaolakexplorer.com), Liquid Liveboards (13/43 Mu 7, Khao Lak, tel. 07/648-5069, www.liquid-adventure.com), and Sea Dragon Dive Center (5/51 Mu 7, Petchkasem Rd., Khao Lak, tel. 07/648-5420, www.seadragondivecenter.com).

Transportation

If you're not going to the islands on a live-aboard, you can take one of the National Parks ferries, which run from September to May. The boat leaves the Thap Lamu Port at 8:30am and takes about 1.5 hours to get to the National Parks headquarters on Similan Island. Boats returning to the mainland depart at 1:30pm. Round-trip fare is 2,700 baht per person.

MU KO SURIN NATIONAL PARK

Mu Ko Surin National Park (tel. 07/647-2145), a group of five islands called the Surin Islands, is about 35 miles from the mainland, due west from Kuraburi. It is known for its impressive coral reefs and Richelieu Rock, a rock pinnacle jutting out of the ocean that attracts whale sharks. These islands are accessible only by live-aboard trips from Phuket, but if you're staying in Khao Lak, you can visit on a day trip.

Beaches and Islands

Ko Surin Nua and Ko Surin Tai, adjacent to each other, are the largest and the most popular of this group of islands. Ko Surin Tai is where the national park office is located, as well as some camping facilities, bungalows, and canteens. Some of the Surin Islands are inhabited by small groups of Moken people who live in a larger group on Ko Surin Tai.

The group of islands is hilly and covered in vegetation. Aside from the excellent coral reefs that fringe some of the islands, they are close enough to each other, and the surrounding waters are shallow enough, that it's possible to walk from Ko Surin Nua to Ko Surin Tai during certain times. Chong Chark Bay, which connects the two, offers stunning views of the islands and surrounding clear water.

Access to both islands is very limited. Visitors are not permitted to wander the island freely. There are no similar restrictions on the open water, though, so your best bet for exploration is by longtail boat tour, which can be arranged through the national park office. You can also rent snorkeling equipment there if you didn't bring your own.

These islands are only open for visitors between November and May; they close completely during the rainy season.

Day Trips

Because the islands are farther north than the Similans, it's only possible to do day trips from Khao Lak. Many diving shops in Khao Lak offer daylong diving and snorkeling trips, including Wicked Diving (4/17 Mu 7, Khao Lak, tel. 07/648-5868, www. wickeddiving.com), Khao Lak Explorer (13/43 Mu 7, Petchkasem Rd., Khao Lak, tel. 07/648-5308, www.khaolakexplorer.com), Liquid Liveboards (13/43 Mu 7, Khao Lak, tel. 07/648-5069, www.liquid-adventure. com), and Sea Dragon Dive Center (5/51 Petchkasem Rd., Mu 7, Khao Lak, tel. 07/648-5420, www.seadragondivecenter.com). These trips will include transport from your hotel to the pier, speedboat or slow boat to the Surin Islands (about 1 hour or about 4 hours), snorkeling and diving, lunch, more snorkeling and diving, and transport back. Rates with most companies start at 3,000 baht for snorkeling and 5,500 baht for diving.

Overnight Trips and Camping

Many diving shops also organize overnight trips to the islands. Accommodations, available through the Department of National Parks, are basic wooden bungalows and cabins with running water and fan cooling. All are located on Ko Surin Tai. Prices are 2,000-3,000 baht per night. Book accommodations with the Department of National Parks (tel. 02/562-0760, np_income@dnp.go.th). Once the reservation is booked, you must transfer full payment to the National Parks by bank wire (or at a Krung Thai Bank or ATM in Thailand).

Tour companies that offer overnight trips to the islands will make arrangements in advance for you. Even if you do make your own arrangements, there is no ferry between these islands and the mainland or Phuket, so you must contact a tour company for transportation.

Live-Aboards

Live-aboards are the best way to see as much of the Surin Islands as possible, especially if you are an experienced diver. The quality and size of live-aboards vary tremendously from tour company to tour company (and the type of boat a tour company uses is not necessarily indicative of the quality of dive instruction or supervision you will get). There are fewer dive companies doing live-aboards to the Surin Islands than the Similan Islands, and nearly all of them are based in Khao Lak. Four such outfitters are Wicked Diving (4/17 Mu 7, Khao Lak, tel. 07/648-5868, www.wickeddiving.com), Khao Lak Explorer (13/43 Mu 7, Petchkasem Rd., Khao Lak, tel. 07/648-5308, www.khaolakexplorer. com), Liquid Liveboards (13/43 Mu 7, Khao Lak, tel. 07/648-5069, www.liquid-adventure. com), and Sea Dragon Dive Center (5/51 Petchkasem Rd., Mu 7, Khao Lak, tel. 07/648-5420, www.seadragondivecenter.com).

Transportation

If you're going through a tour company or travel agent, they will arrange transportation for you and will likely even include transfer from your hotel. If you are trying to get to the Surin Islands on your own, there is a ferry run by the national parks department that runs from September to mid-May and departs daily at 9am from Kuraburi Port, which is about 60 miles north of Khao Lak. The trip takes about 2.5 hours to get to the National

Parks headquarters on Ko Surin Nua. Tickets cost 1,500 baht. Boats returning to the mainland depart at 1pm. Round-trip fare is 1,100-1,700 baht per person. If you go this route, make sure you contact the Department of National Parks (tel. 07/647-2145) to confirm that it is still running before making your plans around it.

In Kuraburi, there are some travel agents who can arrange passage on a speedboat or another vessel making the journey. One such agency is Kuraburi Greenview Travel (www.toursurinislands.com), part of the Kuraburi Greenview Resort (140/89 Mu 3, Kura, Kuraburi, tel. 07/640-1400, www.kuraburigreenviewresort.com).

SI PHANG NGA NATIONAL PARK
อุทยานแห่งชาติศรีพังงา

Mostly rainforest on a rugged mountain range, Si Phang Nga National Park (8:30am-6pm daily, 400B) has the 60-meter-high (197 ft-high) Namtok Tam Nang waterfall and a number of smaller waterfalls. There are a limited number of marked trails in the park; on them are ample opportunities to spot rare birds, including hornbills. There are small bungalows for rent as well as a campground, but this park, unlike most others in the region, does not have a beach. Although the names are similar, this is not the same park as Ao Phang Nga National Park.

Sports and Recreation
There are a few short marked hiking trails in the park. The nicest is actually the shortest, at just over 1.5 kilometers (1 mi), starting at the Tam Nang waterfall. From there, you head up to a viewpoint in the forest where you can see the mangrove swamps edging out into the sea.

Transportation
The national park is located between Kuraburi and Takua Pa on Highway 4. If you're driving, you'll see signs from the highway for the national park and the Tam Nang waterfall. Follow signs for either, as the park's headquarters are right next to the waterfall. The park is east of Highway 4.

Krabi   กระบี่

With a rugged coastline and white-sand beaches, the former fishing area of Krabi is probably the most beautiful province on the mainland of Thailand if you're looking for a beach destination. Like the island of Phuket, Krabi has a mountainous green interior broken up by highlands and some plains as well as an irregular coastline creating lots of small bays and beaches. Right off the coast of Krabi are some of the most beautiful limestone rock formations in the Andaman Sea, which offer great opportunities for rock climbing, if you're feeling adventurous, or sea kayaking through some of the caves worn into the rocks, if you prefer a less strenuous approach. The best beaches in Krabi are located in the center of the province, around Rai Le and Nang, and you'll have to see them to understand just how beautiful a simple beach can be. It's not just the water and the sand, although the crystal-clear blue Andaman Sea and clean, fine sand certainly help. It's the surrounding cliffs and luxuriant tree greenery as well as the view to the small islands off the coast that create a landscape like nowhere else in the world. Krabi Province is also technically home to some of the best islands in region—Ko Phi Phi and Ko Lanta—although many people will travel to these from Phuket or Trang, as they are about halfway between those locations and Krabi. Although Krabi certainly has its share of luxury resorts catering to vacationers' every whim, the region is nowhere near as built up as Phuket is.

Getting to some of the popular beaches involves taking a boat from the mainland—although Krabi is not an island, there are many spots where no roads go. Maybe because it is slightly less accessible, Krabi also has a more rugged feel to it.

KRABI TOWN
เมืองกระบี่

Most people pass through Krabi Town on their way to the beaches or skirt it entirely on their way from the Krabi airport to the boat pier. While there's no reason to stay in Krabi Town unless you're on a really tight budget, as it's not close to the beach and the available accommodations are not quite up to international standards, it's an interesting place to spend a few hours, if only to see what life is like away from the beaches. The town is set on the Krabi River, an estuary that empties into the Andaman Sea farther down, and there are some picturesque wooden houses built on stilts, although you may find some of the town less charming and appealing due to its urbanized feel. Krabi Town does have some of the most interesting and creative statues-cum-traffic lights in Thailand. If that's not enough to hold your attention for very long (they're not *that* interesting), there's also a night market (Khong Kha Rd., right next to the Chao Fa pier, 6pm-10pm daily) where visitors often stop to take photos or grab a snack from one of the curry stalls or *satay* vendors. The Maharat Market, on Maharat Soi 9, opens at 3am and closes by midday daily. It's one of the largest indoor markets in the country, and although you probably won't be taking home any of the seafood or produce on offer, it's worth looking at.

BEACHES
Ao Nang Bay
อ่าวนาง

The large, sweeping Ao Nang Bay is the most popular beach area in Krabi, with scores of accommodations, including many large international chains. Although nowhere near as hopping as Patong, Ao Nang is nonetheless a very touristy, slightly generic resort area. Still, the physical landscape surrounding the bay is impressive—there are scores of different small islands and rock formations in view. Ao Nang also serves as a jumping-off point for day trips to the surrounding islands. Unfortunately, the beach itself is not great for swimming. There is substantial boat traffic, and also no sun chairs or umbrellas available.

Noppharat Thara Beach
หาดนพรัตน์ธารา

Just adjacent to Ao Nang is Noppharat Thara Beach, a long sandy beach that's technically part of a national park. Lined with casuarina trees, the beach used to be quiet and relatively undeveloped, but in recent years it has become increasingly busy and built up. Much of the overflow from Ao Nang spills out onto the southern part of this beach, but the development is creeping north, too. There are accommodations and places to eat here, though it's just a quick ride to Ao Nang. Like Ao Nang, it's not a great beach for sunbathing or swimming, though more and more people seem to be doing it. There are no sun chairs or umbrellas available to rent, and at low tide it can be a long, long walk to the water.

Klong Muang Beach
หาดคลองม่วง

The newest destination beach in Krabi is Klong Muang Beach, north of Ao Nang and Noppharat Thara. The beach is more remote than either, but that is changing quickly, as high-end hoteliers have "discovered" it and are building luxury resorts in the area. The beach itself isn't great for swimming. It can be very shallow depending on the tides and is also rocky in places. Still, if you want to be on the water and enjoy a relatively secluded experience, take a look at some of the accommodations options here.

★ Rai Le Beach
หาดไร่เลย์

The small Rai Le Beach, surrounded by limestone cliffs behind and large rock

Krabi Beaches

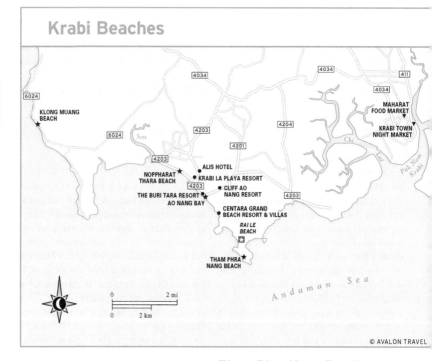

© AVALON TRAVEL

formations rising from the sea in front, is the most beautiful of the beaches in Krabi and arguably one of the most beautiful in all of Thailand. Since Rai Le is an isthmus jutting off the mainland, there are actually two Rai Le beaches, one to the east and one to the west. With crystal-clear blue waters and soft sand, **West Rai Le** is both breathtaking and totally relaxed. **East Rai Le** also has lovely surrounding scenery, but it's actually mostly mudflats, and there's no sand and nowhere to lay out a towel. But that's not a problem, as you can easily walk to sandy West Rai Le in 10-15 minutes if you're staying on the east side, where accommodations are generally less expensive. Rai Le's beauty has not escaped the rest of the world's attention. More hotels have sprung up in spots where it seemed impossible to build, and it has become a destination for day-trippers doing tours of the region. Although it is still as beautiful as it always was, it's much less peaceful, especially during midday.

Tham Phra Nang Beach
หาดถ้ำพระนาง

Just a short walk from Rai Le at the end of the peninsula, the small, secluded **Tham Phra Nang Beach** is bordered by a rocky headland on one side and limestone cliffs on the other. There's also a mystical cave here—**Tham Phra Nang Nok,** or Princess Cave—believed by local fisherfolk to house a sea princess. Although so far she hasn't been sighted by any travelers, you can check out the interesting offerings that are left for her in the cave. This beach is also a day trip destination, and during the day it can be literally overrun.

SPORTS AND RECREATION
Rock Climbing

Krabi has the best rock climbing in the country, thanks to the beautiful limestone mountains and the built-up rock-climbing industry. There are hundreds of bolted routes that will take you as high as

300 meters (984 ft) at varying levels of difficulty. This is not a sport to try without some training or proper equipment, but fortunately there are at least half a dozen rock-climbing shops offering lessons, rentals, and guided tours. Total beginners can take either full-day (2,000 baht) or half-day (1,000 baht) lessons, which include on-the-ground training and climbing. Those with experience can either hire a guide to explore the many routes in the area or just rent the necessary equipment and pick up a map from any of the shops.

Wee and Elke of **Basecamp Tonsai** (Ton Sai Beach, next to Ton Sai Bay Resort, www.basecamptonsai.com), formerly Wee's Climbing School, literally wrote the book on rock climbing in Krabi. You can buy their newly updated guide at their shop or take one of the half-day, full-day, or multiday classes they offer. Their shop also sells and rents an extensive selection of equipment. **Hot Rock** (Rai Le Beach West, tel. 07/562-1771, www.railayadventure.com) is also highly recommended because of the professionalism and personalities of their guides. They offer instruction for beginners and tours for advanced climbers. Their shop also sells and rents equipment.

Kayaking

The uneven coastline, mangrove forests, and scores of rock outcroppings and islands make Krabi an excellent area to explore with a kayak. Many guided kayaking tours (around 1,500 baht for a full day) leave from Ao Nang. On a typical tour, you'll spend some time paddling through the nearby mangrove forests and also set out to explore some of the small islands and sea caves that have been created through thousands of years of erosion. **Sea Canoe Thailand** (Ao Nang, tel. 07/569-5387) is one of about half a dozen companies offering daily kayak tours.

On Rai Le Beach West, there are rental kayaks available right on the beach (400 baht for the day). Inexperienced kayakers should be aware that currents can be surprisingly strong and that longtail boats, speedboats, and larger vessels are frequently in the water and may not see you.

Snorkeling

The islands around Krabi, including **Ko Phi Phi,** have some of the best snorkeling in the country, and it's quite possible to see not only amazingly colorful tropical fish and coral gardens with just a snorkel and a mask, but you might even spot some reef sharks. While

Rai Le Beach, Krabi

many people choose to enjoy snorkeling on one of the day tours offered by dive shops and travel agents in Krabi, it is also possible to charter a longtail boat to take you out on your own. If you're going the prepackaged-tour route, Kon-Tiki Thailand Diving & Snorkeling Center (61/1 Mu 2, Ao Nang, tel. 07/563-7675, www.kontiki-krabi.com) offers snorkel-only excursions (850 baht) instead of the usual boat tour of the area with snorkeling tacked on. Their tours will take you to Ko Phi Phi and the Mu Ko Hong islands, and since they're focused on snorkeling you'll spend as much time as possible in the water.

If you'd prefer to go out on your own, longtail boats can take you out to the smaller islands around Ao Nang and will generally know where you'll be able to see fish or coral. There are scores of private longtail captains in Ao Nang and West Rai Le available; prices for personalized trips are entirely negotiable, but you should expect to pay at least 1,000 baht for a few hours on the sea. Longtail boats are smaller, less comfortable, and slower than speedboats (and life preservers are generally nonexistent), so if you are planning on going out on one, it's best done for shorter distances.

rock climbing in Krabi

ACCOMMODATIONS
Ao Nang

If you want to avoid the big properties, The Buri Tara Resort (159/1 Mu 3, Ao Nang, tel. 07/563-8277, www.buritara.net, 3,500B), with only 69 guest rooms, is a smart, stylish choice in the budget-luxury category. The pool isn't as large as what you'll find at other resorts, and it's a few minutes' walk to the closest beach, but the property opened at the end of 2006 and the guest rooms are nicely decorated in a modern dark-wood style with some Thai touches.

The small, charming Alis Hotel (125 Ao Nang, tel. 07/563-8000, www.alisthailand.com, 2,500B) has a unique Mediterranean design and comfortable guest rooms with luxurious baths. For nice guest rooms and a good location about 10 minutes from the beach, it's a good choice. There's a nice rooftop pool and

a bar on the premises, but the grounds aren't massive, and the lack of things such as elevators are a reminder that it's not quite a boutique resort but rather a small hotel.

Although not as beautifully kept up as the Centara Grand, the large Krabi La Playa Resort (143 Mu 3, Ao Nang, tel. 07/563-7015 to 07/563-7020, www.krabilaplaya.com, 5,100B) has a great pool area and roomy, well-furnished guest rooms done in a modern Thai style. It is right on the beach and an easy walk to town. Some of the guest rooms have swim-up access to the pool.

The Cliff Ao Nang Resort (85/2 Mu 2, Ao Nang, tel. 07/563-8117, www.thecliffkrabi.com, 8,000B) is a beautiful property with many design elements from traditional bungalows but completely modern, comfortable guest rooms. Although there are some rustic elements, they're purely aesthetic—there's not a trace of backpacker to be found. The semioutdoor baths are spacious and have rain showerheads, the restaurant is elegant, and the pool is large and minimalist so as not to detract from the natural beauty found in the surrounding cliffs and ocean. This is definitely a hip, romantic resort designed for couples, although kids are welcome.

The Centara Grand Beach Resort and Villas (396-396/1 Mu 2, Ao Nang, tel. 07/563-7789, www.centralhotelsresorts.com, 8,000B) has large, beautiful guest rooms with stunning ocean views, top-class resort amenities, and excellent service, all set on its own small private bay with a small beach right next to Ao Nang. If you don't feel like leaving the compound, there are five different places to eat within Centara as well as a spa and multiple swimming pools. If you're looking for a big resort experience in Krabi, this is probably the best price you'll find in the category, and especially in the off-season, when you'll pay about half the price; it's a bargain.

Noppharat Thara

Sunda Resort (19 Mu 3, Noppharat Thara, tel. 07/566-1262, www.sundaresort.com, 1,200B) has all the basics a traveler would want in a small resort—a swimming pool, small on-site restaurant, decent buffet breakfasts, and clean, modern rooms. The Sunda Resort is surprisingly stylish for a three-star resort, though because of limited facilities it is not in any way a luxury property. To get to the beach, you'll need to walk about 15 minutes; there is also a hotel shuttle available.

For a slightly more upscale resort, try the Baan Habeebee (25 Mu 5, Noppharat Thara, tel. 07/566-1210, www.baanhabeebee. com, 4,000B), also about 10 minutes on foot to the beach and a short shuttle bus ride to Ao Nang. The mostly wooden structures on this leafy resort have a tropical island feel, as does the pretty swimming pool. Most of the standalone bungalows have big sitting porches, too. This is a halal resort, so there is no beer served. It is also close to a local mosque, so you will hear the call to prayer starting early in the morning.

Klong Muang

Nakamanda Resort (126 Mu 3, Klong Muang, tel. 07/756-8200, www.nakamanda. com, 4,000B) is a new all-villas resort on Klong Muang. It has a great location on the beach, right across from a small uninhabited island (you can even walk there during low tide). The villas and common areas are designed in a Mediterranean-meets-Balinese style, with clean, white buildings topped with terraced roofs. Inside the rooms, the decor is subtly tropical and inoffensive. The large swimming pool looks out onto the beach, though it's not a great one for swimming. Staff is attentive and friendly.

The Phulay Bay, A Ritz-Carlton Reserve (111 Mu 3, Klong Muang, tel. 07/562-8111, www.ritzcarlton.com, 10,000B) is undoubtedly the most luxurious resort in the area. Rooms are palatial (the smallest are about 800 square feet) and include all the amenities one would expect at a Ritz-Carlton—flat-screen TVs, massive bathrooms, DVD players, free Wi-Fi, and minibars. Some have small private pools overlooking the ocean. The rooms are bright and airy with lots of traditional Thai elements. The common spaces make full use of the region's beautiful woodwork. The location, on a small bump of beach on Klong Muang, is very secluded, though it's still only 10 minutes by car to Ao Nang.

Rai Le Beach

Since it's set on the mudflats side of Rai Le, you'll have to walk about 15 minutes to get to the good part of the beach from Sunrise Tropical Resort (39 Mu 2, Ao Nang, Rai Le Beach, tel. 07/562-2599, www.sunrisetropical.com, 3,500B), but it is a great value if you want to stay in a well-appointed beach bungalow without paying five-star resort prices. The bungalows are modern, spacious, and clean, the baths have outdoor showers and are nicely fitted, and the grounds are leafy. The larger villas are enormous for the price. Although it's a small property with only 28 bungalows, there's a pool, a small restaurant, and an Internet café.

If you can get one of the bungalows at ★ Railei Beach Club (Rai Le Beach, Ao Nang, tel. 07/562-2582, www.raileibeachclub. com, 5,000B), consider yourself lucky. A cluster of houses set right on the beach, this is neither a resort nor a hotel. Each of the homes is individually owned and rented out by owners when they're not in town, and they vary in size from cozy bungalow to four-bedroom house. The design of each is a little different, but they're all wooden bungalow houses with clean, comfortable bedrooms and baths. Some have elegant dark-wood furnishings; others are a little more rustic. The larger buildings have their own kitchens and entertaining space, perfect for a family or larger group, or a couple that wants to spend an extended time. There's no pool, although it is set on what is arguably the most beautiful part of the beach. Although it's not a resort, there's daily maid service, and if you want, they'll arrange to have someone come to your bungalow and cook dinner for you.

"Beach bungalow" doesn't do the Rayavadee Premier (214 Mu 2, Ao Nang, tel. 02/301-1850, www.rayavadee.com, 15,000B) justice. The individual accommodations are more like small luxury homes set in a quiet, secluded part of the beach. This is one of the most indulgent places to stay on Rai Le, as is clear from the hefty rates you'll pay. The property has nearly 100 bungalows, so there are lots of amenities, including tennis courts, a fitness center, and a handful of restaurants. While most people staying on Rai Le have to arrive at the pier on the east side of the beach and walk to their resort, the Rayavadee will arrange to have a private boat pick you up from Krabi Town and deliver you straight to the resort. Despite the high prices, peak season fills up months in advance, so book quickly if you're interested in staying here.

FOOD
Krabi Town
Hands down the best Thai restaurant in Krabi Town, both for food and ambience, is ★ Ruen Mai (315/5 Maharat Rd., tel. 07/563-1797, 11am-10pm daily, 200B). It may be filled with travelers, but don't be put off. It's worth feeling like a lemming to enjoy a meal in this verdant garden setting. The curries and other typical Thai dishes are well executed, but for something different, try the crunchy *plai sai* fried fish snacks or *kaeng som* sour curry with fish. This is also a great place for vegetarians. Although there aren't many straight veggie offerings on the menu, the kitchen will prepare just about anything you want without meat.

For a distinctly southern-Thailand breakfast dish, head to Kanom Jin Mae Weaw (137 Krabi-Khao Thong Rd., next to the PTT gas station, tel. 07/561-2666, 7am-noon daily, 50B) for some *kanom chin*—curry served over thin rice noodles. This very casual place has three different varieties and serves them spicy. For Western palates it may feel more appropriate to have this for dinner, but it's a morning meal, so get there early to try it.

Ao Nang
For seafood on the beach, Wangsai Seafood Restaurant (98 Mu 3, Ao Nang, tel. 07/563-8128, 10am-10pm daily, 300B) is a good relaxed restaurant with a view of the ocean and a large deck right on the beach. The large sign is in Thai (it's the only place with no English sign), but the menu has English translations for all the typical Thai seafood dishes, including seafood fried rice and braised fish in lime, chilies, and garlic. The restaurant is quite popular among foreign visitors.

Another popular, solid choice for seafood on the beach is the Salathai Restaurant (32 Mu 2, Ao Nang, tel. 07/563-7024, 9am-10pm daily, 300B). The menu has both traditional Thai dishes with seafood and some Western fare. Better to stick with the local food and seafood, which you can select yourself, and enjoy the view at this charming thatched-roof restaurant right on the water. It's not very fancy, by any standard, but the food and location are just right.

Krua Thara (82 Mu 5, Ao Nang, tel. 07/563-7361, 11am-9:30pm daily, 200B) has great seafood dishes, whether part of a traditional Thai meal or just plain grilled or fried with Thai sauce. Like most of the places to eat in Krabi, it's nothing fancy to look at, but the food is good.

Rai Le Beach

While Rai Le has some of the best beachfront property in Thailand, it's definitely not a contender for best dining options; Krabi Town and Ao Nang have much better dining. That's not to say the food is bad, but there isn't much selection—most of it is from bungalow and resort restaurants and the roti vendors on the beach in the afternoon.

TRANSPORTATION

When planning your trip, remember that Krabi Town is more than 16 kilometers (10 mi) away from the area's main attraction—the beaches. You'll likely want to head to Ao Nang, as that's where most accommodations are and where you can catch a longtail boat to one of the outer beaches or islands.

Air

The Krabi Airport (tel. 07/563-6541) has frequent flights from Bangkok and is served by Thai Airways and Bangkok Airways as well as the budget airlines Nok Air, Air Asia, and One-Two-Go. If you're coming in from Singapore, Tiger Airways also has direct flights from that city. Although the airport is comfortable and modern, it's very small, and the services inside, including food, are very limited.

From the airport, it's about a 30-minute drive to Ao Nang; there are plenty of taxis on hand to take you (400-600 baht). There is also a private airport shuttle that runs at least every hour (more frequently during high season) between the airport and Ao Nang. The fare is 150 baht, so if you're traveling with a group, it can be more economical (and faster if you happen to be staying at the last hotel on the route) to take a taxi.

It's also possible to fly into Phuket International Airport and then make the three-hour drive to Krabi. There is a minibus from the Phuket airport that goes to Krabi Town. It leaves three times daily 9am-1pm for 350 baht per person.

Boat

From Phuket, there is a boat that heads to the Noppharat Thara pier next to Ao Nang at 8am daily and goes back to Phuket at 3pm. The ride is about two hours and costs 350 baht.

Boat connections between Phi Phi and Krabi are frequent, especially during high season. There are ferries from Noppharat Thara pier that are currently running once daily at 3pm. The ride is about three hours and costs 550 baht. To get to Krabi from Phi Phi, there are frequent boats during high season, leaving at 9am, 10:30am, and 2:30pm.

If you're on Phi Phi, there are also ferries that leave Phi Phi at 9am for Ao Nang in Krabi and take a little under three hours.

If you are coming from Ko Lanta, boats only run during high season; otherwise, you'll have to take a minivan, which involves two short ferry crossings. During high season, ferries from Ko Lanta to Krabi leave at 8am and 1pm daily, returning at 10:30am and 2:30pm. The cost is 300 baht per person and takes about 1.5 hours.

Even if you're coming by air or ground transportation to Krabi, if you're staying in Rai Le, you'll have to take a boat to get to your ultimate destination. Although Krabi is on the mainland, there are no roads to Rai Le; you have to take a longtail boat from Ao Nang or Krabi Town. There are frequent boats from the Saphan Chaofa pier that should run around 80 baht per person (unless you arrive after the scheduled boats have stopped running, in which case you will have to negotiate with the owner of the boat). Your hotel in Rai Le will be able to arrange the transfer for you. The short trip to Rai Le can be a little treacherous, depending on the weather conditions and what you're carrying. The boats stop on East Rai Le beach, and if the tides are in when you arrive, the pier may be partially submerged in water. You have to walk, carrying your luggage, through sometimes knee-deep water, so it is essential that you pack only what you can comfortably lift over your head while walking. Once you get onto dry land, if you're staying on West Rai Le, you'll need to walk about 15 minutes to get to your final location. There are no cars or motorcycles—another reason to pack light. If you happen to be staying at the Rayavadee, they'll arrange a private boat to take you directly to the hotel—they'll even carry your stuff for you.

Bus

There are overnight buses leaving from Bangkok's Southern Bus Terminal at 5:30pm daily for the 12-hour overnight drive to Krabi. Tickets on air-conditioned luxury buses cost 850 baht and terminate in Krabi Town. Regular air-conditioned buses leave Bangkok at 7am, 4pm, and 5:30pm daily and cost 450-600 baht. There are also frequent buses to Krabi from Phuket, Ko Pha-Ngan, Surat Thani, Trang, and Hat Yai.

Car

It's relatively easy to drive to Krabi. Highway 4, which runs south down the peninsula, is the best way to go and is well signed in English for the correct turnoff to Ao Nang. Once you're in the area, many people find cars totally unnecessary, as most time is spent either on the beach or at one of the many marine sights that can't be reached by road anyway.

THAN BOK KHORANI NATIONAL PARK
อุทยานแห่งชาติธารโบกขรณี

Mostly mountainous rainforests and mangroves, the small Than Bok Khorani National Park (8:30am-6pm daily, 400B) also has a number of ponds, caves, and streams that seem to disappear under the limestone mountains as well as, of course, sandy beaches. There are also more than 20 small islands, really just rocks jutting out of the ocean, that are a part of the park. The best way to visit the islands is by canoe or kayak, but most do not have beaches, so it's difficult

to disembark. Camping is allowed in the park, but amenities are very limited, so you'll have to bring everything with you.

Inside the park is the cave Tham Phi Hua To, which is believed to have been a shelter for prehistoric people living in the area; it has some prehistoric paintings of people and animals. The cave got its name, which means "big-headed ghost cave," because of the number of abnormally large human skulls found in the cave. It is also used by Buddhist monks as a temple and for meditation retreats. The cave is not accessible by land; to visit you have to take a boat. If you aren't already exploring the area by boat, or just want to visit the cave, you can pick up a longtail boat to take you there from the Bo Tho pier in Ao Luek.

Transportation

If you're staying in Ao Nang, you can get to the park either by land or by sea. It's a one-hour drive to the Bo Tho pier in Ao Luek, where you'll be able to either rent a canoe or kayak or charter one of the local boat captains to take you around. If you don't have a car, you can charter a longtail boat from Ao Nang to take you to the park and tour you around the islands (expect to pay around 1,000 baht for the trip, regardless of the number of passengers), making it a great day trip if you're hanging out in one of the more touristed areas in Krabi.

KHAO PHANOM BENCHA NATIONAL PARK
อุทยานแห่งชาติเขาพนมเบญจา

Another small national park worth visiting for a few hours because of the waterfalls and peaks is Khao Phanom Bencha National Park (8:30am-6pm daily, 400B). There are some short hiking trails, including one that will take you to the highest point in the area, at more than 1,200 meters (3,937 ft), and another that will bring you to a three-tiered waterfall called Namtok Huay To, where the water collects into 11 large pools at the base. The Tham Khao Phueng cave has stalagmites and stalactites typical of caves in the region.

You can pick up a map of the park at the ranger station; the trails are easy to moderate.

Transportation

Less than 32 kilometers (20 mi) from Krabi Town, Khao Phanom Bencha National Park is best accessed either by car, *tuk tuk,* or motorcycle. If you get a ride from Krabi Town or Ao Nang, it's better to arrange round-trip transport, since when you're done exploring the park, there may not be anyone around to bring you back. If you are driving, take Pracha U Thit Road north out of Krabi Town, until you see Ban Thap Prik Health Center, where you take a left and continue heading north to the ranger station.

KHLONG THOM
คลองท่อม
Sights

The Khlong Thom hot spring (10B pp) is worth a visit if you happen to be in the area, particularly for the so-called Emerald Pool, where springwater collects in the forest, creating a strangely deep emerald or turquoise color, depending on the time of day. To see the pool at its best, come when the light is soft, either very early in the morning or just before dusk.

Right near the Emerald Pool is the Ron Khlong Thom waterfall, in a part of the forest with lots of small hot springs that flow into cold streams, creating a warm-water waterfall.

The Khao Pra-Bang Khram Wildlife Sanctuary (เขตรักษาพันธุ์สัตว์ป่า เขาประ-บางคราม, 8:30am-6pm daily, 200B), also commonly referred to as Khao Nor Chuchi, has some small trails through lowland forests and past the Emerald Pool. The sanctuary is considered the single richest site for birds in the whole region, and you're likely to

spot black hornbills and kingfishers. Gurney's Pitta, of which there are less than 100 pairs estimated to exist on the planet, are known to nest in this area. There is also camping in the sanctuary, although unlike the national parks, there are no tent rentals, so you have to come equipped.

If you're interested in archaeology, the Wat Khlong Thom Museum (Mu 2, Petchkasem Rd., Khlong Thom, tel. 07/562-2163, 8:30am-4:30pm daily, free) at Wat Khlong Thom houses numerous items found during an excavation of Kuan Luk Pat, commonly referred to in English as the bead mound. Items on display include tools from the Stone and Bronze Ages, pieces of pottery, coins, and colored beads said to be more than 5,000 years old.

Transportation

To get to Khlong Thom, drive on Highway 4 heading south from Krabi Town; Khlong Thom will be marked at the junction of Highway 4 and Route 4038. From there, you will see well-marked signs directing you to the Emerald Pool or the wildlife sanctuary. You can also take a public bus headed for Trang from the bus terminal outside Krabi Town and tell the driver when you board that you want to get off at Khlong Thom. These buses run nearly hourly during the day, and you'll spend less than 30 baht to get to Khlong Thom. You'll end up in a small town area and will have to find transport to the surrounding sights, but during the day there are plenty of motorcycles that will take you. Although you can sometimes find a ride back from the sanctuary or the Emerald Pool, it's best to arrange round-trip transport at least back to Khlong Thom, where you can catch a bus heading for Krabi or Trang for the rest of your journey.

In recent decades it seems the rest of the world has discovered what residents and intrepid travelers knew all along—the Ko Phi Phi islands, a small group of islands in Krabi Province about 40 kilometers (25 mi) off of the west coast of the mainland and just south of Phang Nga Bay, are lush and beautiful, the surrounding waters warm and clear, and the marinelife astounding. The discovery may have something to do with the Leonardo DiCaprio movie *The Beach,* which was filmed in the area. Certainly the movie helped put the islands on the map, but it's the physical beauty and ease with which you can go from lazing around on the beach to snorkeling or scuba diving that will make sure it stands the test of time.

The largest island of the group and the only one with tourist accommodations, Ko Phi Phi Don is shaped like two separate islands connected together by a thin strip of land with sandy beaches on each side. The beaches along that isthmus, Ton Sai Bay on the south and Loh Dalam Bay on the north, have become very popular for day-trippers and those staying on the island. The island is only about 16 kilometers (10 mi) long, and there are no roads or motorized transportation to take you from one part to another. Instead, there are plenty of longtail boats that function like shuttle buses and taxis. The rest of the islands in the group can easily be visited via a short ride on a longtail boat taxi from Phi Phi Don, or on a longer two-hour ferry or tour boat if you're coming from Phuket or Krabi.

Originally inhabited by Muslim fisherfolk, Phi Phi Don has changed dramatically in recent years. Ton Sai Bay is jam-packed with restaurants and small shops selling everything from sunglasses to T-shirts. Where there were once only a few simple bungalows, there are now full-scale resorts with swimming pools, spas, and anything else a traveler might be interested in, although in a much lower-key manner than you'll see on Phuket. If you're visiting Phi Phi or one of the surrounding islands for the day, you'll notice scores of speedboats and ferries moored close to the shore, all bringing in visitors who can crowd the beaches during high season. Residents and enlightened guests do their best to keep the island clean, but at times you will notice some wear and tear from the hundreds of visitors who come to the island every day. It's a shame, because Phi Phi is probably one of the most beautiful islands in the Andaman region, and it increasingly feels like its beauty is on the edge of being spoiled by overly eager tour operators and irresponsible visitors.

Neighboring, smaller Ko Phi Phi Le is a stunning limestone island encircling emerald-green Maya Bay. There are no accommodations on Phi Phi Le, but it has become a huge tourist draw, with day-trippers visiting by the hundreds per day during high season. With the throngs of other people and scores of motorboats in the bay, it's amazing that the island continues to look as beautiful as it does.

BEACHES
★ Ton Sai Bay
หาดต้นไทร

The beaches along **Ton Sai Bay,** including **Hin Khom Beach** and **Long Beach** (Hat Yao), are stunningly beautiful, with white sand and mountain ranges off in the distance as well as some great opportunities for viewing the coral just off the coast. This beach area, however, is the most popular, and right behind the beach there are scores of guesthouses, bungalows, and even some bars and shops. If you want a budget backpacker experience in paradise, this is where you'll probably end up. This is also a popular place for day visitors to hang out, meaning it can become very crowded during high season.

Ranti Beach
อ่าวรันตี

Off the east coast of the larger part of Phi Phi Don, Ranti Beach has fewer accommodations and can only be reached from Ton Sai Bay on foot, or by speedboat or longtail, so pack light if you are planning on staying here. The beach itself is as beautiful as the rest of the island, and there is plentiful coral to view right off the coast. If you're looking for budget bungalows but want to avoid Ton Sai, Ranti is a great place to stay.

Phak Nam Beach
อ่าวผักหนาม

Phak Nam Beach has the same clear blue water and soft sand as Ranti, but is even more secluded, with very few accommodations, though this will probably be changing soon in light of all the development going on in the region. To get to this beach, you can either hike to the east side of the island or take a water taxi.

Laem Thong Beach
หาดแหลมตง

Way at the northern tip of the island, Laem Thong Beach is one of the quieter areas, with a long white-sand beach and only a few accommodations. This area, at a point when the island thins out to only about 200 meters (656 ft) wide, has a quiet, peaceful atmosphere and a handful of high-end resorts. It can be a little difficult to get to if you're coming from Ton Sai Bay, as it's too far to walk, and you have to travel by water, but the beach has its own pier, so you can skip the crowds and commotion and head straight here from the mainland instead.

Ko Phi Phi Le
เกาะพีพีเล

On Ko Phi Phi Le there are no accommodations but some beautiful places to visit either from the mainland or from Phi Phi Don. Amazing emerald water and large rock formations characterize Maya Bay (อ่าวมาหยา), a tiny bay on the east side of Phi Phi Le. Once you enter the bay, you'll be astounded by the beauty of the surrounding physical landscape. There's a small beach for swimming with rocky outcroppings overhead and even a tiny bit of rainforest to walk around in. There are no overnight accommodations on Maya Bay, but the place gets packed with day-trippers, so try to arrive early to enjoy a bit of the beauty without the crowds. You can go by longtail boat or speedboat, or paddle over on

view from Ko Phi Phi

your own. The bay itself is not great for snorkeling (especially because it's usually filled with boats), but if you walk across the island and through a small cave (you can't miss it, as there's only one path you can walk on), there's some better snorkeling off of that coast, including views of sea urchins and tropical fish.

Monkey Beach (Hat Ling, หาดลิง) is a fun place to visit if you want to hang out with the scores of monkeys populating this pretty little strip of sandy coast that can be reached by canoe, speedboat, or longtail boat. If you go, make sure you bring something for the monkeys to snack on—as a result of thousands of tourists visiting every year, they've grown to expect some compensation in exchange for the entertainment they're providing, and they can get a little surly and even aggressive if you disappoint them.

SPORTS AND RECREATION
Diving

Phi Phi has some of the best diving in Thailand, made even better by the fact that it's so accessible and inexpensive. There's no need to set out on a boat for days or even to stay on Phi Phi. With all of the organized dive trips from Phuket, you can easily schedule full-day trips and return to the main island at night. Most of the outfitters listed for the Andaman coast offer trips to Phi Phi. There are more than a dozen certified PADI dive shops on Phi Phi; check the PADI website (www.padi.com) for information about them. Four companies that offer diving trips off Ko Phi Phi are Wicked Diving (4/17 Mu 7, Khao Lak, tel. 07/648-5868, www.wickeddiving.com), Khao Lak Explorer (13/43 Mu 7, Petchkasem Rd., Khao Lak, tel. 07/648-5308, www.khaolakexplorer.com), Liquid Liveboards (13/43 Mu 7, Khao Lak, tel. 07/648-5069, www.liquid-adventure.com), and Sea Dragon Dive Center (5/51 Mu 7, Petchkasem Rd., Khao Lak, tel. 07/648-5420, www.seadragondivecenter.com).

Boating

Most of the boating that goes on around Phi Phi is through chartered speedboats that take visitors from island to island during the day. These trips are hugely popular, as evidenced by the number of charter boats that line the coast of Phi Phi. Many of these tours include some snorkeling as well as lunch and depart from either Phi Phi or Phuket. There are a handful of companies that offer tours, although they sell almost exclusively through third-party tour agents, and you can arrange a tour through any travel agency on the mainland or Phi Phi, or from your hotel. Because of the intermediaries, prices for the trips can vary and are negotiable, although the agent may not tell you that it's not actually their company putting together the package. Prices for a day trip around Phi Phi should run about 1,200-2,000 baht, depending on the type of vessel you're on and the number of other passengers.

If you want to cruise around the surrounding islands at your own pace, at almost any beach you can hire a longtail boat to take you from one place to another. It's quite an experience to sit back and take in the view of the Andaman Sea from one of the long, thin, colorful boats while the captain steers from behind. Compared to speedboats, longtail boats are a lot smaller and less agile in choppy waters, so they're best enjoyed if you're only doing limited island-hopping. When longtail boats are used as taxis, prices are usually fixed, and you should expect to pay 40-100 baht per trip. Chartering a boat for a fixed amount of time can cost anywhere from 400 baht, depending on the number of people and the time of year.

Kayaking

The area around the Phi Phi islands offers excellent opportunities for sea kayaking to explore the hidden bays and mangrove forests surrounding the islands. If you're just looking to paddle around close to shore, there are plenty of kayaks on the beaches available for rent. Experienced kayakers can rent kayaks and arrange to have them pulled by longtail from Phi Phi Don to Maya Bay on Phi Phi Le, which costs around 300-500 baht. You can also request that the boat's captain pick you up at a designated time and place when you're ready to return. It's possible to cross from one island to another by kayak, but weather conditions can change rapidly, and only experienced kayakers should attempt the venture.

If you're kayaking, bear in mind that Phi Phi is a very popular destination for speedboats and larger tour boats, and by midday in high season the whole area can get very crowded with larger vessels. What may seem like just an annoyance can become dangerous if you're not seen by another boat, so pay close attention to the waters around you. The quietest time for kayaking is early in the morning, before the rest of the world arrives.

ACCOMMODATIONS

Phi Phi Don was long a favorite of travelers on a budget, thanks to the cheap bungalows, especially along Ton Sai Bay, that had few amenities but the prime real estate on the island. The island was devastated during the tsunami in 2004, and most of the bungalows, resorts, and hotels have had to rebuild. Like everywhere else in Thailand, tourism is moving upscale, and the rebuilding seems to have shifted the island's focus from budget backpacker upward. Although there are still opportunities to sleep in a small shack on the beach without air-conditioning or hot water for just a few hundred baht per night, you'll find those accommodations increasingly packed together in smaller and smaller areas (namely Ton Sai), with midrange hotels and more expensive resorts popping up on the island in their place. On the luxury front, the island is increasingly getting its share of high-end resorts, too. Perhaps because Phi Phi is so beautiful and so popular, hoteliers don't seem to be trying too hard to compete with one another or to woo guests. The most common complaint that travelers have about the island is that where they stayed was overpriced and mediocre, regardless of whether it was a cheap bungalow or a high-end resort.

Ton Sai Bay

With scores of guesthouses in the area, Ton Sai Village, the small strip of flat land in the middle of the island, is a popular spot for visitors to stay. Here's where you'll find most conveniences; the majority of the island's restaurants and small shops are here, but you'll find less peace and calm.

J. J. Guesthouse (Ton Sai Village, tel. 07/560-1090, www.jjbungalow.com, 700B) offers very basic fan-cooled guest rooms in its small guesthouse. Guest rooms are clean and comfortable, and definitely good value for the money. There is a small restaurant on the property. For a little more money, you can stay at one of the bungalows, which are all air-conditioned and spacious, though simple.

Viking Natures Resort (222 Mu 7, tel. 07/581-9399, www.vikingnaturesresort.com, 1,200B) has old-fashioned wooden bungalows in a rustic, lush setting about 20 minutes on foot from Ton Sai Village. Rooms are basic wooden structures nestled in the trees. They are fan-cooled and because they're not airtight, you have to rely on a mosquito net at night to keep critters out. Larger bungalows have space for lounging and can sleep up to six people. Some parts of this resort are louder than others at night, so make sure you state your preference when you reserve.

JJ Residence (95 Mu 7, tel. 07/560-1090, www.jjresidence.com, 1,500B) is a small hotel in Ton Sai Village on the side farthest from Ton Sai Bay. Rooms are modern, clean, and comfortable, and there is a nice small swimming pool on the grounds. This is a good choice for those who want to stay right in the center of the action, but it can get loud and hectic here even during the day as it is right next to the market.

If you want to stay right near Ton Sai Bay but still feel a little pampered, the Phi Phi Island Cabana Hotel (58 Mu 7, tel. 07/560-1170, www.phiphi-cabana.com, 4,200B) is a nice choice for a not-too-expensive resort. The guest rooms are well maintained, and the grounds are nicely designed. The guest rooms are all decorated in a modern Thai style and feel much less rustic than bungalows you'll find scattered along the beach, and there's a nice large swimming pool with comfortable chairs. The hotel is also very well located on Ton Sai between two beaches, so visitors can take advantage of the more inexpensive longtail boats in the area to hop from place to place. The only trade-off is that with more than 150 guest rooms, it's not quite a small resort.

Laem Thong Beach

At the northern tip of the island, in secluded Laem Thong Beach, is Phi Phi Natural Resort (Mu 8, Laem Thong Beach, tel. 07/561-3010, www.phiphinatural.com, 3,300B). The standard guest rooms and cottages have a rustic feel to them, with lots of exposed wood and simple, basic furnishings. It's nothing luxurious or fancy, but there's air-conditioning and a small swimming pool with an ocean view. The resort is tucked away from any crowds and feels secluded and relaxed, more like a summer vacation at camp. There are also larger cottages that are great for families.

For something a little more predictable, if with slightly less personality, the Holiday Inn Phi Phi Island (Mu 8, Laem Thong Beach, tel. 07/562-7300, www.phiphi.holidayinn.com, 4,000B) has nice individual bungalows, many with ocean views. The swimming pool is not huge but opens onto the beach. Bungalows are decorated in a modern, somewhat generic style but have some small Thai details. Many have their own small balconies or porches.

The least expensive option on this part of the island is the three-star P.P. Erawan Palms Resort (Mu 8, Laem Thong Beach, tel. 07/562-7500, www.pperawanpalms.com, 2,500B), a pretty, midsize resort with standard rooms and stand-alone bungalows. Rooms are modern, clean, and pretty, with basic wood furnishings and modern bathrooms. The little swimming pool overlooks the beach, which is usually quiet and uncrowded.

Ao Lo Bakao

This beach's only resort, Outrigger Phi Phi Island Resort and Spa (Ao Lo Bakao, tel. 07/562-8900, www.outrigger.com, 6,500B), is definitely on the higher end of the beach bungalow experience, although it's not quite a five-star luxury resort. The bungalows and villas are done in a traditional Thai design with thatched roofs that fade into the surrounding palm trees and are designed to let in as much light and ocean view as possible. There are a spa and a few restaurants on the premises as well as a fantastic swimming pool looking out onto the Andaman Sea. This is a great place to stay if you're looking for seclusion and are happy to idle your vacation away reading books and listening to the waves, although at low tide the shore is too rocky and shallow to swim. Getting off the resort during the day can be a little tricky—the resort has infrequent shuttle boats running to Ton Sai Bay, but if you miss them and need to charter a private boat from the hotel, the prices are steep.

Ao Toh Ko

Ao Toh Ko Bungalows (Ao Toh Ko, Phi Phi Island, tel. 08/1731-9470, 350B) offers supercheap, basic sleeping accommodations with lovely beach views in a quiet, secluded beach on the east coast of the island. If you're on a budget, or just want to experience what Phi Phi was like before all the other travelers came, these little bungalows will feel charming and quaint, and the little bar and inexpensive restaurant on the premises will feel like an added extra. If you're higher maintenance, this is not the place for you, however: There's no air-conditioning or hot water in most of the guest rooms.

FOOD

Come nighttime, Ton Sai Bay is ground zero for food and entertainment, and if you're staying on one of the more remote beaches, the action can be a welcome change from all that peace and quiet. Almost all of the resorts on the island have small restaurants serving Thai food. Western food tends to be more than well represented at the stand-alone shops, perhaps to feed all the hungry Americans, Europeans, and Australians who flock here.

Even if you'll feel a little guilty eating baked goods on a tropical island, ★ Pee Pee Bakery (Ton Sai Bay, 7am-8pm daily, 40B) is hard to resist. The shop's glass display cases of doughnuts, breads, and cakes seem to beckon every traveler, especially around breakfast time. The bakery also serves Thai food, sandwiches, and pizza, all of which are well prepared.

During the day, the seafood restaurants right on the edge of the beach overlooking Ton Sai Bay are usually filled with day-trippers on arranged tours. At night, these restaurants feel less like food conveyer belts and are pleasant places to drink a cold Singha over dinner and enjoy the view. Chao Koh (tel. 07/560-1083, 11am-9pm daily, 250B) is one with good seafood and a nice view. Cuisine here is traditional Thai seafood dishes. The food is good, but don't expect anything too creative.

Anna's Restaurant (111 Mu 7, tel. 085/923-2596, 7:30am-9pm daily, 250B) in Ton Sai Village is something of an institution in Phi Phi, though the menu is just basic Thai food, with some Western/European dishes, and drinks (nothing out of the ordinary for Thailand). Service is consistent and reliable, and it's a big enough restaurant that you can almost always get a table. If you just want an easy place to sit and eat decent food, you won't be disappointed here.

Hidden behind the Outrigger Resort in Loh Ba Gao is this tiny casual Thai place, Knock Out Bar (Loh Ba Gao, tel. 087/278-7901, 11am-9pm daily, 200B), owned by a family that also runs longtail boat tours of the island. The bamboo bar and thatched roof feel just right after a long day of island-hopping, and the food is mostly good, basic Thai food that's freshly prepared. This is also a fun place to hang out and have a drink, as everyone is very friendly and relaxed.

Le Grande Blu (Ton Sai Village, tel. 081/979-9739, 11am-10pm daily, 600B), a small French and Thai fusion restaurant, is considered by some to be the best restaurant on the island. The pretty, all-wood dining room is just a step nicer than most nonresort restaurants here. And whether you want to try the excellent European fare or prefer to stick with Thai food, the quality of the food and service are also a step above. Western desserts, including profiteroles and crème brûlée, will really hit the spot if you are craving a bit of non-Thai food! This is Ko Phi Phi, so don't expect a fine dining experience; you won't be refused service if you show up in shorts.

Although some visitors, particularly the over-30 crowd, seem perplexed as to the reason, Hippies (Hin Khom Beach, tel. 08/1970-5483, 8am-late daily, 200B) is a wildly popular restaurant, bar, and party spot right on Hin Khom Beach. The menu, which features Middle Eastern food, pizza, and plenty of Thai dishes, seems designed to offer something for everyone. The food is actually pretty good (although if you want authentic Thai food, make sure to ask for it extra spicy), but it's really the beachfront location, charming thatched roofs and bamboo furniture, and laid-back vibe that are the draws here.

TRANSPORTATION
Getting There

The only way to get to the island is by water. In the past, intrepid tour operators have tried using seaplanes for the short flight from Phuket airport, but they have not managed to make that business model work.

Phi Phi Don is easily reached by ferryboat or speedboat from Phuket or Krabi. There are no public ferries per se, only private operators, and when you buy a ticket, most will include a ride from your hotel in Phuket or Krabi to the pier. Schedules change frequently, especially in the low season, but during high season there are at least two boats from Chalong Bay in Phuket to Ton Sai Bay on Phi Phi Don, one in the morning and another in the afternoon, and returning boats on a similar schedule.

The trip should take around two hours, depending on the weather conditions. From Krabi, there are boats leaving from Ao Nang and Rai Le Beaches daily, also in the morning and afternoon. Fares run from 350 baht upward, depending on the time of day and the season. If you're with a large group of people, it can sometimes be more economical to charter your own speedboat from Chalong Bay or Krabi to Phi Phi. In a small, fast vessel, the trip can take half as long as the larger boats, but you should expect to pay a few thousand baht per journey.

Given the cost of the trip, if you have some time to spare, it may be worthwhile to take one of the package tours that will not only bring you to Phi Phi but also provide a tour of neighboring islands and sights while you're on the way. Just make sure the boat will stop at Ton Sai Bay (if that's where you're going), as some tours skip this spot entirely.

Many of the hotels on Phi Phi can arrange your transport from either Krabi or Phuket for you if you're staying on their property. Otherwise, you can buy tickets from any travel agent, but when purchasing, make sure to ask about the size of the boat and the number of passengers if you have a preference for the type of vessel. Larger ferries and speedboats generally take 90 minutes from either Krabi or Phuket. During the low season, it's fine just to show up at the pier and buy a ticket, but during high season ferries can sometimes sell out, so the best bet is to find a travel agency and buy a ticket as soon as you can.

Getting Around

There are no taxis or *tuk tuks* on Phi Phi; for the most part there aren't even any roads. Most of the getting-around involves walking or traveling from Ton Sai Bay to other spots on the island by longtail boat, the area's taxi service. You'll pay 40-100 baht per person per trip from one part of the island to another, depending on the distance and whether you are traveling alone. From one island to another, expect to pay around 100 baht per person for the boat trip. Your hotel will be able to arrange a boat for you, but if you're picking one up from the beach, make sure you agree on the cost in advance.

Ko Lanta   เกาะลันตา

Just off the coast of Krabi is Ko Lanta, really two adjacent islands—Ko Lanta Yai and Ko Lanta Noi. Ko Lanta Yai, generally referred to just as Ko Lanta, is a large, thin island with limestone cliffs, a jungly interior, mangroves, and some good coral beaches. Although there are mangroves along much of the coast, there are also some great sandy beaches on the west side of the island, and that's where you'll find plenty of bungalows and small resorts. The interior has some great hiking trails through rainforests and some waterfalls worth checking out in Lanta's national park, which covers nearly half the island. Ko Lanta is arguably nearly as blissfully beautiful as Phi Phi, but Ko Lanta has yet to explode with the same popularity as its neighbor, and

it has a strange half-backpacker, half-luxury vibe to it that some visitors find a perfect balance. You'll see this interesting dichotomy in the choice of accommodations as well—there are some great choices at both the upper and lower ends. Ban Saladan, a small village on the northeast corner of the island, functions as Ko Lanta's Main Street. This is where many of the ferries arrive, and there are also some limited amenities such as ATMs, Internet cafés, and supermarkets, but some of the more popular beach areas will have similar amenities as well. Ko Lanta Noi, adjacent to Ko Lanta Yai, has no beaches and has therefore not become a big destination, but depending on how you get to Ko Lanta, you may end up passing through the island.

SIGHTS
Lanta Old Town
หมู่บ้านเก่าแก่เกาะลันตา

Located on the east side of southern Ko Lanta, Lanta Old Town is a quaint fishing village that now serves as the island's capital. It's picturesque, with little teakwood houses on stilts above the water and brightly colored fishing boats set against the backdrop of an enticing blue ocean speckled with islands that seem to emerge as you watch. But Lanta Old Town is also a fascinating place to observe the cultural diversity in southern Thailand that's often difficult to discern in heavily touristed areas. The town, once a major fishing port in the middle part of the 20th century, is home to Chinese immigrants, descendants of nomadic seafarers, and Thai Muslims who've created a comfortable, peaceful town blending all of their cultures together.

BEACHES AND SURROUNDING ISLANDS
★ Khlong Dao Beach
หาดคลองดาว

Khlong Dao Beach, closest to Ban Saladan, is a long stretch of wide, sandy beach on the southwest tip of the island backed by casuarina and palm trees. The waters in this crescent-shaped beach are generally quite calm, but this is the island's most popular tourist spot, so expect more of everything—more accommodations, more places to eat, and more people. It's still Ko Lanta, though, so even during peak season, you won't see any overcrowding at Khlong Dao.

Pra Ae Beach
หาดพระแอะ

Pra Ae Beach (also called Long Beach) is another stretch of wide, sandy beach, with a nice selection of bungalows and resorts right on the water nestled among the trees. Just a few kilometers down from Khlong Dao, Long Beach is rarely crowded.

Khlong Khong and Khlong Nin Beaches
หาดคลองโขง และ หาดคลองนิน

As you move farther down the island, there are still plenty of bungalows right on the coast, but the beaches become less crowded with accommodations and people. Both Khlong Khong and Khlong Nin Beaches are served by a little village called Ban Khlong Nin, where you'll find all the basics, including an ATM, some places to eat, and small shops.

Kan Tiang Bay and the Southwest Coast
อ่าวกันเตียง

With less usable beach in relation to mangrove or rocky shore, this is where the island starts to feel remote. Kan Tiang Beach, located within the bay of the same name, with its white sands and just a scattering of resorts, is nearly deserted in the low season, making it a great choice if you're looking for a quiet, romantic getaway. Mai Pay Bay is sometimes nicknamed "Last Beach" because it's at the end of the island and feels like the last beach in Thailand that hasn't been discovered. With simple bungalows and little going on other than the beautiful scenery and warm blue waters, Mai Pay Bay feels off the beaten path, and it attracts the backpacker crowd and other adventurers seeking scenery as well as peace and quiet.

Ko Ha
เกาะห้า

A group of five small rocky islands off the coast of Ko Lanta, Ko Ha is a popular place for diving and snorkeling due to the abundant coral and exotic sealife surrounding the islands as well as the excellent visibility in the water. There are no accommodations on the island, but it's often visited on day trips. To get to Ko Ha, you'll need to charter a speedboat or sailboat or go with an organized tour.

Ko Hai (Ngai) Lanta
เกาะไหง

With just a handful of resorts and very limited amenities, Ko Hai Lanta offers the quintessential desert-island experience if you're willing to give up a few luxuries in exchange. The small island, mostly hilly rainforest, has a stretch of beautiful beach with views of karst rock formations rising from the sea and some great coral snorkeling just off the coast. The island is in Krabi Province just south of Ko Lanta Yai, but it's more convenient to get there by taking a boat from Trang instead. If you're staying on the island, the resort will arrange transportation for you.

Ko Ta Lebeng and Ko Bu Bu
เกาะตะละเบ็ง และ เกาะบูบู

Off the east coast of Ko Lanta, Ko Ta Lebeng is a limestone island with dramatic limestone cliffs and lush mangroves as well as a small bit of sandy beach. The island is very popular among sea kayakers and is a great place to go if you're not confident in open waters—the smaller Ko Ta Lebeng is protected by the main island, and the waters are a little calmer.

If you want to stay on a small island, Ko Bu Bu has only one resort with a handful of bungalows and clear warm waters for snorkeling. "Chilled-out" might be too exciting to describe the place—there's some great sandy beach and not much else to occupy your time other than sitting in a hammock and reading a book. The island is even too small for any long hiking.

NIGHTLIFE

Club Ibark (Khlong Nin Beach, Ko Lanta Yai, tel. 08/3507-9237, 6pm-late daily, no cover) bills itself as the country's freshest and funkiest club and, while that's definitely not true, it is the hottest thing going on Ko Lanta. Of course, Ko Lanta is a small island, and the nightlife pickings are pretty slim. Still, during high season the club pulls in a good crowd, and the DJs spin music that's head and shoulders above the typical Western pop classics you'll hear at most venues. There's a casual, fun vibe at this open-air dance club, and since everyone is on vacation, the partying can go on 'til late at night.

SPORTS AND RECREATION
Ko Lanta National Park

Ko Lanta National Park covers Hat Hin Ngam and Hat Tanod Beaches at the southern tip of Ko Lanta as well as a handful of surrounding small islands and rock formations. There are no resorts on the beaches, and like the other national parks with beaches, there are some camping amenities. Tanod Beach, at the bottom of Ko Lanta, is covered in rugged mountain terrain and sugar palms, giving way to a beautiful beach. There are hiking trails throughout this area filled with birdlife, and at the end is the Lanta lighthouse, where you can climb up and view the island from above.

There are campgrounds as well as many bungalows that can be rented from the parks authority. Approaching the lighthouse and surrounding area by road can be really tough without a 4WD vehicle, and depending on the weather, it may be easier to charter a longtail boat to take you.

Snorkeling

If you're looking to do some serious snorkeling, the area surrounding Ko Lanta has some great coral reefs and marinelife to see. You can swim out on your own, but to really see what's going on in the sea, arrange a boat trip around the island and neighboring islands. Freedom Adventures (70 Mu 6, Khlong Nin Beach, Ko Lanta Yai, tel. 08/4910-9132 or 08/1077-5025, www.freedom-adventures. net) runs group day trips for about 1,500 baht from Ko Lanta on its charming wooden motorboat and can also create a personalized itinerary for you depending on your interests and abilities. This is a great excursion for nondivers who are interested in seeing the coral and tropical fish, as these folks specialize in snorkeling and not diving, so they'll only take you places you can enjoy viewing the underwater world without need of breathing gear.

ACCOMMODATIONS
Under 1,500B

Bu Bu Island Resort (Ko Bu Bu, tel. 07/561-8066, 350B) is a throwback to the days when simple bungalows on quiet beaches dominated the now mostly built-up Andaman coast. Guest rooms are very basic thatched-roof bungalows with private cold-water baths. There's also a small restaurant here, making it a great place to just chill out and enjoy the view.

1,500-3,000B

If you want to pay backpacker prices but don't want to forgo things such as a swimming pool and a restaurant on the premises, the Andaman Lanta Resort (142 Mu 3, Khlong Dao Beach, Ko Lanta, tel. 07/568-4200, www.andamanlanta.com, 2,100B) is a decent midrange option. The guest rooms are clean, if a little weary, but the resort is relaxed and child-friendly. Located on the north part of the island, it's definitely in a more crowded neighborhood, but the nearby beach stays mellow even during high season. It sort of looks like a group of IHOP restaurants, since all of the buildings have similar blue roofs.

Right nearby, at the southern end of Khlong Dao Beach, Lanta Villa Resort (14 Mu 3 Saladan, Ko Lanta, tel. 07/568-4129 or 08/1536-2527, www.lantavillaresort.com, 1,900B) is a similar property with clean, basic guest rooms and a nice swimming pool right on the popular beach. The bungalow-style rooms are a little too close together to feel secluded, but for this price and this location, it really is a bargain.

Ancient Realm Resort & Spa (364 Mu 3 Saladan, Ko Lanta, tel. 08/7998-1336, www.ancientrealmresort.com, 1,800B) is a solid midrange beach resort with excellent service and good-value guest rooms. Some might be aesthetically offended by the liberal use of Buddhist and Southeast Asian images in the decor, but if you can get past that, the guest rooms are very comfortable and clean, and the beach location is excellent. All guest rooms have air-conditioning and hot water. The resort also feels less businesslike than some other properties, so staff and guests are more relaxed and friendly.

LaLaanta Hideaway (188 Mu 5, Ko Lanta, tel. 07/566-5066, www.lalaanta.

com, 2,800B) is quiet, secluded, and relaxing, and though the bungalows are not at the five-star level, they are clean, nicely furnished, and comfortable enough that you won't miss much. There is a hotel restaurant and bar, plus a large swimming pool overlooking the Andaman Sea. The beach the resort is located on feels very secluded, and those who are looking for a place that feels like a deserted island will enjoy their time here.

3,000-4,500B

The small Baan Laanta (72 Mu 5, Kan Tiang Bay, Ko Lanta Yai, tel. 07/566-5091, www.baanlaanta.com, 3,500B) resort has only 15 bungalows, which straddle the line between rustic and luxurious. Terra-cotta tiles and lots of wood and bamboo give the guest rooms a very natural feeling, but things like a minibar, bathrobes, and private balconies with excellent views add bits of pampering and indulgence. The dark-tiled pool, spa *sala* (pavilion), and outdoor bar are small but swanky-feeling and well maintained.

A boutique resort of the best kind, ★ Sri Lanta (111 Mu 6, Khlong Nin Beach, Ko Lanta Yai, tel. 07/566-2688, 3,800B) is both aesthetically pleasing and geared toward connecting visitors to the beautiful surroundings of Ko Lanta. This is not a place designed to make you forget where you are: The individual thatched-roof villas have wall-length shutters that you can open out onto the grounds, and the interiors are rustic but comfortable and deliberately don't have TVs. But things like the amazing black-tiled swimming pool, Wi-Fi, and good iced coffee mean you won't feel like you're missing out on much during vacation.

Over 4,500B

With bright, beautiful guest rooms set on a property that creeps into the surrounding rainforest along with lots of things to do, the Rawi Warin Resort & Spa (139 Mu 8, Ko Lanta, tel. 07/560-7400, www.rawiwarin.com, 7,800B) has more personality and charm than most large resorts. The guest rooms are modern but have an airy, clean tropical style to them, and the stucco exteriors give the resort a more Mediterranean feel than a Southeast Asian island feel. Some of the gigantic villas have their own swimming pools, but the common areas, which include multiple swimming pools, tennis courts, and a gym, are more than sufficient to keep you occupied. One of the restaurants also has free Wi-Fi. The property is very child-friendly, although some of the guest rooms are located up in the hills and will require a little bit of walking.

If you're looking for more amenities, the ★ Pimalai Resort (99 Mu 5, Ba Kan Tiang Beach, Ko Lanta, tel. 07/560-7999, www.pimalai.com, 12,000B) is a larger property with more than 100 guest rooms nestled in the hilly rainforest above a beautiful, quiet stretch of white-sand beach. All of the guest rooms are in small bungalow buildings, giving the property a less crowded feeling despite the fact that there may be hundreds of guests and staff around during peak season. Inside, the guest rooms are a little more generic but still have some nice Thai design elements. The 35-meter (115 ft) infinity swimming pool overlooking the ocean is nearly as beautiful as the beach below.

FOOD

If you're just looking for casual food, you'll find lots of roti vendors around, selling the traditional Muslim rolled and flattened pancakes. They're traditionally served with savory curries, but these guys will stuff them with all sorts of sweet treats, including chocolate and bananas, for around 30 baht.

Gong Grit Bar (Khlong Dao Beach, 176 Mu 3, Saladan, Ko Lanta, tel. 08/9592-5844, 8am-10pm daily, 300B) is one of the many places you'll find on Khlong Dao Beach serving up local fare and seafood dishes on the beach. This one isn't very fancy—none of them are—but the food is well done and the service is good. Gong Grit is at the southern end of the beach.

TRANSPORTATION
Getting There
BOAT

During high season, there is a twice-daily ferry from Krabi's new pier on Tharua Road, just outside Krabi Town. Remember that there are two piers in Krabi: Chao Fah pier, which is now used for travel immediately around Krabi, and the new pier, which is used for larger vessels. The ferry for Lanta leaves at 8am and 1pm, takes about 90 minutes, and costs 300 baht. It's best to arrange transport to the pier through your hotel in Krabi. There are also daily boats during high season from Ko Phi Phi to Ko Lanta, departing at 11:30am and 2pm daily. That trip takes 90 minutes and also costs 300 baht.

BUS

Although Ko Lanta is an island, you can do much of the journey there by land, using two ferry crossings that can accommodate vehicles. In the low season, this is the only option, and there are numerous minivan services that will take you from Krabi to Ko Lanta. If you take one of the scheduled vans with Lanta Transport (tel. 07/568-4121), which run every few hours and take about 90 minutes, you'll pay 250 baht per person. You can also arrange to have a private minivan with any tour company, which should cost around 1,000 baht.

CAR

If you're driving to Ko Lanta, head south on Highway 4 toward Trang (if you're coming from the Phang Nga area). Turn off at Route 4206 at Khlong Thom, about 32 kilometers (20 mi) from Krabi Town, and follow that road heading south all the way to the Hua Hin pier on the mainland. That leg of the journey is about 29 kilometers (18 mi). From there you'll take your first ferry crossing to Ko Lanta Noi. The second ferry, about 8 kilometers (5 mi) after the first, will bring you to Ko Lanta Yai; each will cost 100 baht.

Getting Around

Ko Lanta does not have a public

transportation system; to get around you'll have to rely on occasional motorcycle taxis and the shuttle buses and trucks run by the island's resorts. If you're driving on your own, by car or motorcycle, the island has a main road on the west coast that runs north-south and will allow you access to those beaches.

Trang and Satun Provinces

จังหวัดตรัง และ จังหวัดสตูล

The two southernmost provinces on the Andaman coast before Thailand becomes Malaysia, Trang and Satun have not yet become popular tourism destinations, although direct flights from Bangkok to Krabi and Trang make them readily accessible for those looking for something off the beaten path. Both share much of the topography of neighboring Krabi—limestone cliffs, beautiful beaches, mangrove swamps, and a verdant interior—but are less commonly visited by travelers, most likely due to the plethora of amazing places to see so close to Phuket and its well-maintained tourism infrastructure. If the idea of flying into a big international airport and staying in a place where you'll most definitely see other foreign travelers is unappealing, these two provinces are worth the extra effort it takes to get here, if only for the chance to see what Thailand is really like while at the same time enjoying beautiful beaches and islands. The provinces are home to some spectacular small islands off the coast, most protected by two large national marine parks and easily accessible from the mainland either for day trips, if you're in a hurry, or extended stays, if you're looking for a desert-island experience. Off the coast of Trang is the Mu Ko Phetra National Park, comprising about 30 islands you can dive and snorkel around, or enjoy the gray-white sandy beaches and do some bird-watching. Off the coast of Satun are the Tarutao Islands, which, compared to their northern neighbors, are more visited, although still nothing like what you'll see in Phang Nga Bay. The national park comprises more than 50 islands where you can see coral and go snorkeling and scuba diving.

The mainland also has its share of natural beauty, and although there are scant tourist sights to see, there's still plenty to keep you busy should you decide to stay here for more than a day or two. Trang was the first area in Thailand where rubber trees, now an important part of the economy of the south, were planted, and Satun is home to a majority Muslim population, making both provinces culturally and historically interesting places to visit in addition to their physical beauty.

Compared to Phuket or Krabi, you won't find the same number or quality of accommodations on the mainland of either Trang or Satun, although a couple of resorts have sprung up in the area as well as some very budget, very simple beach bungalows.

TRANG
Trang Town
เมืองตรัง

Trang Town isn't so much a tourist town as just a small town going about its daily business: Although there are travel agencies that can set up dive expeditions to the nearby islands, hardware stores and noodle shops are the rule instead of tailor shops and bars. It's not a physically beautiful town, and most travelers will see it only in transit from the mainland to the beaches, but if you're interested in what semiurban life looks like in this part of the world, it's a pedestrian-friendly place where you can wander around for a while observing the mundane without fear of getting lost. While it's sometimes difficult to discern small cultural differences among regions in

Trang and Satun Provinces

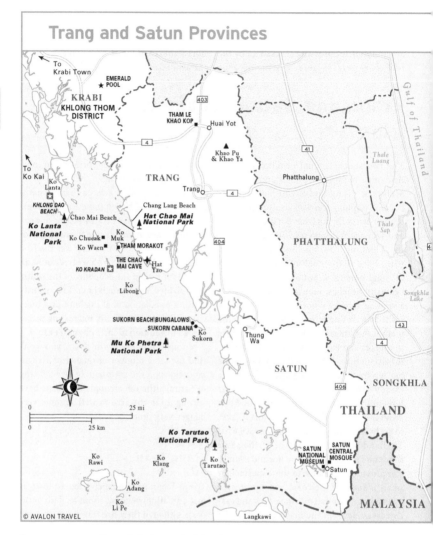

© AVALON TRAVEL

foreign countries, Trang feels distinctly different from more northern areas of Thailand. Like other parts of southern Thailand, the distinct mix of Thai-Chinese and Malay cultures can be fascinating to observe, plus there is some Sino-Portuguese architecture. Other than that, there isn't too much to see except for the markets and the governor's house, set on one of the area's hills.

Here you'll also find some of the best coffee shops. Say goodbye to instant and order a *kopi* instead. Just like the coffee you'll find in cafés in Malaysia and Singapore, this is the strong cloth bag-filtered version with a generous helping of sweetened condensed milk to make it go down smoothly. Trang is also known for two other culinary specialties—dim sum, which you can find at many coffee shops and which is especially popular for breakfast, and *mu yang Trang,* Trang-style crispy roasted pork. Ton Noon Dim Sum (202 Pad Sathani Rd., 6am-9pm daily, 30B) and Khao Chong Coffee (Phatthalung Rd., tel. 07/521-8759, 6am-9pm daily, 30B) are two traditional *kopi* shops with excellent dim sum choices.

Nok Air is the only airline offering flights to Trang from Bangkok, currently leaving from Don Muang airport. If you book far enough in advance on Nok Air, tickets are as cheap as 2,800B round-trip with tax. Otherwise, you may pay a little under 4,000B for a ticket.

There's an overnight train from Bangkok to Trang that leaves Hua Lamphong Station at 5:05pm and arrives in Trang at 7:55am the next day. The tickets cost under 800 baht for a first-class sleeper ticket, so if you're comfortable sleeping on trains, it's a really economical and adventurous way to get to the region.

There are buses for Trang that leave the Southern Bus Terminal in Bangkok around 6pm; call tel. 02/435-1199 for the latest schedule. Buses take 12-14 hours. Expect to pay in the neighborhood of 800 baht for a ticket on an air-conditioned luxury bus, less than 550 baht for an unair-conditioned bus.

If you're driving from the surrounding areas, Highway 4 cuts through Trang in a zigzag pattern, making it the most accessible route for inland travel in the province. For the beaches in the southern part of the province, however, you'll have to turn onto secondary road 404. Although Trang is close to Phuket, Krabi, and Phang Nga as the crow flies, the drive can take hours due to the mountainous terrain. The drive from Krabi Town to Trang takes two hours; from Phuket to Trang, it takes 4.5-5 hours, so plan accordingly.

Mu Ko Phetra National Park
อุทยานแห่งชาติหมู่เกาะเภตรา

Mu Ko Phetra National Park, a marine park in Trang, is a small grouping of islands just north of the Ko Tarutao area that feels even more remote than the rest of the province. The scenery, including the craggy limestone rock formations jutting out from the ocean and rainforest-covered islands, is spectacular. Under the surface of the sea surrounding many of the islands there's coral at relatively shallow depths, making this a great destination for snorkeling. The only way to stay in the national park is either to camp or to rent one of the national park bungalows on Ko Phetra.

Ko Khao Yai means "large mountain island." Although that could adequately define many of the islands in the Andaman Sea, Ko Khao Yai stands out because, thanks to erosion and tectonic forces, one of the large chunks of limestone jutting off the island has been worn through and forms a sort of natural bridge that can be rowed under during low tide.

The much smaller Ko Lidi, which covers less than 10 square kilometers (4 sq mi), doesn't have great beaches for swimming, but it has some caves within the limestone cliffs that are nesting grounds for swallows, along with a campground where you can rent tents.

Accommodations through the Department of National Parks are basic bungalows and dormitory-style rooms with running water and fan cooling. Some are located right on the water. There is also a campground where you can pitch a tent. Prices are 600-1,500 baht per night. Book accommodations with the Department of National Parks (tel. 02/562-0760, np_income@dnp.go.th). Once the reservation is booked, you must transfer full payment to the National Parks by bank wire (or at a Krung Thai Bank or ATM in Thailand). There is a small canteen and restaurant at the park headquarters.

The closest major city to Ko Phetra is Hat Yai, which is about 60 miles away. From Satun, the park is about 35 miles. If you are driving from Hat Yai, take Highway 4 north to Route 406. When you hit the beginning of Route 416, follow that road until you see signs for the park. There are also public buses that run from Satun to the park. You'll need to check the schedule at the Satun bus station (intersection of Route 406 and Sulakanukoon Soi 17).

Ko Muk
เกาะมุก

Just off the coast of Trang, across from

Chang Lang Beach, Ko Muk is a small inhabited island with some beautiful beaches backed by limestone cliffs on the west coast, coral clusters to snorkel around (particularly nearby Hat Sai Yao), and a scattering of bungalows and resorts catering to travelers. To the south, the eastern part of the island is mainly a fishing village, and the local economy is also dependent on the rubber plantations in the center of the island. But to the north, on the west coast, lies one of the coolest physical attractions in the region—the Tham Morakot (Emerald Cave). If you visit during low tide, you can access the cave and interior lagoon by boat, but the more fun way to go is during high tide, when the entrance to the cave is nearly filled with water and you have to swim through the limestone passage. When you reemerge, you'll be in a beautiful emerald lagoon surrounded by cliffs. During high season this is a popular place, so don't expect to have it to yourself.

To get to Ko Muk, you can take a longtail or speedboat from the Kuan Tungku pier, which is about 30 minutes from Trang Town. If you're flying into the Trang airport, there are frequent *song thaew* traveling this route during the day; expect to pay around 50 baht per person. At the pier, you'll have to negotiate with the captain, but a trip to Ko Muk will take around 30 minutes on a longtail boat and will cost around 400 baht.

Hat Chao Mai National Park
อุทยานแห่งชาติหาดเจ้าไหม

The Hat Chao Mai National Park (Mu 5, Ban Chang Lang, Amphoe Sikao, tel. 07/521-3260, 8:30am-6pm daily, 200B) is a large protected area covering 19 kilometers (12 mi) of rocky and sandy coastline north of Hat Yao and south of Krabi Province. The interior of the park includes mangrove swamps, mountains, and rivers. The park also technically extends to the adjacent islands of Ko Muk, Ko Kradan, Ko Waen, Ko Cheaung, Ko Pring, and Ko Meng, although you won't necessarily notice that you've entered the park or even have to pay an entrance fee if you're visiting one of these islands. Although the park is a beautiful nature preserve and includes some amazing coral reef offshore, what Hat Chao Mai is best known for is the dugong, or sea cows, that live in the ocean territory covered by the park. This endangered species, similar to a manatee, was once hunted but has now been adopted by the locals as the region's unofficial mascot. The sweet, awkward-looking dugong can sometimes be spotted during snorkeling or diving trips along the coast or islands covered by the park. If you're looking to explore the mainland part of the park, there are simple bungalows for rent as well as areas to camp with restrooms and canteens serving up tasty, casual local food.

★ Ko Kradan
เกาะกระดาน

Partially under the protection of the Hat Chao Mai National Park, Ko Kradan is often called the most beautiful island in Trang. It's no surprise, given the beautiful view of Ko Muk and other neighboring islands that seem to emerge magically from the Andaman Sea, the pristine soft-sand beaches, and the surrounding coral reefs. For snorkelers it's particularly alluring: The water is clear, and you'll only need to swim out to shallow depths to see some amazing coral and tropical fish. Although there are some rubber plantations on the island, it's largely undeveloped and usually visited by tourists as part of a tour to Ko Muk. If you want to stay over, there are a few bungalows on the island, and you can also camp on the island through the parks department.

Hat Yao and Surrounding Islands
หาดยาว

The longest stretch of beach in the province, Hat Yao has some clear sandy swaths punctuated by rock formations and rocky cliffs backed by pine and palm trees. Off the coast in the warm, clear-blue waters of the Andaman Sea are some islands and rock formations where you'll be able to do some snorkeling and diving away from the crowds a little farther north. There are very limited accommodations on the beach; it's definitely quiet and secluded. For budget travelers it's a great option if you feel like you've been squeezed out of the more popular tourist areas as they've gone upscale—you can still find accommodations for less than US$15 per night in the area.

Just off the coast of Hat Yao is Ko Libong. The largest island in Trang is a very short trip by longtail boat from the pier at Yao Beach and has a handful of small fishing villages and rubber plantations populated by the mostly Muslim Thais living in the area. The island itself has some beautiful sandy beaches and rugged, hilly rainforest in the middle, and there is snorkeling right off the coast, although not as much coral to be seen as you'll find in and around Phi Phi. Ko Libong also has a handful of quaint resorts if you're looking to stay on the island overnight.

South of Ko Libong is Ko Sukorn, one of the southernmost islands in Trang Province. This island has a handful of small villages mostly engaged in fishing and working on small rubber plantations on the island. The brown sandy beaches are surrounded by clear waters, and the island is mostly flat and without many of the rock formations characteristic of the region. The island is small enough that you can walk around it in a few hours, and close enough that it only takes about 20 minutes in a longtail boat from the mainland; you'll get a chance to see how people in the region make a living while enjoying the laid-back atmosphere on the island.

There are some relaxed bungalow resorts here, although nothing is fancy. If you're looking for an off-the-beaten-path island getaway, this is a great place to stay for a few days. Sukorn Beach Bungalows (Ko Sukorn, tel. 07/526-7707, www.sukorn-island-trang.com, 1,000B) is casual and unpretentious. This is definitely a place to stay for the location and the price, and for now you won't have to worry about being overrun by other travelers, since Ko Sukorn hasn't made it big yet. The guest

rooms are filled with simple bamboo furniture and are a very short walk to the beach; most have air-conditioning. There aren't many amenities available here, but there is a small restaurant serving Thai food.

Sukorn Cabana (Ko Sukorn, tel. 07/511-5894, www.sukorncabana.com, 1,000B) has airy, basic, but pretty bungalows. This is not a high-end resort—many of the bungalows don't have air-conditioning or hot water—but they're just minutes from the beach.

Ko Chueak and Ko Waen, just adjacent to each other off the coast of Trang, are two very small islands with some of the best casual snorkeling in the region. Aside from some exotic, colorful fish, there is plenty of deep- and shallow-water coral to view.

On the mainland, the national park area covers Khao Pu and Khao Ya mountains, which have thick forest cover, caves, and plenty of waterfalls to hike around in. Tha Le Song Hong—Lake of Two Rooms—is a fascinating and beautiful physical phenomenon to view. The large, clean lake is nearly divided by a mountain rising from the middle, creating two separate bodies of water. To get there by car, take Petchkasem Road (Huai Yot-Krabi) to Ban Phraek, then turn right and drive about 13 kilometers (8 mi). There will be signs in English pointing the way. If you want to rough it a little, there's a Boy Scout campground (tel. 07/522-4294) nearby. When it's not filled with kids, they rent out the houses.

Chang Lang Beach
หาดฉางหลาง

Chang Lang Beach has all of the spectacular scenery typically found along the Andaman coast—limestone cliffs, sandy beaches, and casuarina pine trees. One of the campsites, as well as the main headquarters for Hat Chao Mai National Park, is located on the beach.

At the tip of a forested headland is Chao Mai Beach, a wide stretch of sandy beach covering about three kilometers (2 mi) of coastline. Both of these beaches are beautiful and feel much more remote and less populated by visitors than the national parks to the north; if you come during the low season, you may well be the only person around.

The Chao Mai Cave is one of the larger caves in the region, with extensive stalactites and stalagmites, fossils, and multilevel chambers. There's also a spring inside one of the chambers, and some of the stalactites and stalagmites have joined, creating strange-looking pillars and an altogether otherworldly feeling inside. Although the cave is on the grounds of the national park, it's easier to access from Yao Beach. From here, you can rent a rowboat to row into the cave from the ocean.

Another cool cave to visit is Tham Le Khao Kop, which has pools of water and a stream flowing through it as well as steep interior cliff walls, plus more than three kilometers (2 mi) of stalagmites and stalactites. During the day there are guides who'll row you through the cave in a little boat. At one point the passage is so low you have to lie on your back in the boat, which feels like an adventure. To tour the cave with a boat and guide, the fee is 200 baht per boat or 30 baht per person. Take Highway 4 from the Huai Yot district heading toward the Wang Wiset district (อำเภอวังวิเศษ). After about six kilometers (4 mi), you will see Andaman intersection; continue for 460 meters (1,509 ft), and you will see another intersection with a temple on the right; turn left, drive about 640 meters (2,100 ft), and you'll see a bridge to the cave.

SATUN
Satun Town
เมืองสตูล

As untouristed as Trang Town is, Satun Town is even more so. The center of the southernmost province on the Andaman coast before Malaysia, the town of Satun, as with the whole province, is primarily Muslim, having been a part of Malaya until the early 19th century. Sectarian violence has infected the three southernmost provinces on the east side of the peninsula, but even though Satun is nearly right next door, there have been no reports of insurgent activity here, and it's a great opportunity to catch a glimpse of a culture

different from what you'll see to the north. To better understand Islam in Thailand, visit the Ku Den Mansion, the Satun National Museum. Housed in a colonial-style former palace that once housed King Rama V, this museum for Islamic studies has interesting displays on the lives of Muslims in the area through the ages. There's also the large Satun Central Mosque. Although it's not going to win any architectural awards, having been completed in the late 1970s, you can visit to pray or watch others do so.

If you're heading to Satun, you can take a train to Hat Yai (there's no train station in Satun), but then you have to travel by land for the remaining 95 kilometers (59 mi).

Satun is on the same bus line as Trang. Buses leave the Southern Bus Terminal in Bangkok around 6pm; call tel. 02/435-1199 for the latest schedule. Buses will take 12-14 hours to reach Satun. Expect to pay in the neighborhood of 800 baht for a ticket on an air-conditioned luxury bus, less than 550 baht for an unair-conditioned bus.

If you're driving through Satun, Route 416 travels down the coast slightly inland, and from there you'll turn off onto country roads depending on your destination. Although Satun is close to Phuket, Krabi, and Phang Nga, keep in mind that the drive can take hours due to the mountainous terrain. If you are driving from Krabi Town to Satun, it will take three hours. From Phuket to Trang, the drive will take 5.5-6 hours.

Ko Tarutao National Park
อุทยานแห่งชาติหมู่เกาะตะรุเตา
Ko Tarutao National Park in Satun is the highlight of the region if you're looking for a place to do some diving and snorkeling. The park comprises more than 50 islands off the coast of Satun and just north of Malaysian territorial waters, some barely a speck on the map and some, such as Ko Tarutao, covering dozens of square kilometers of land. Within the island group you'll find rainforests, clean quiet beaches, mangroves, coral reefs, and plenty of wildlife. The park headquarters (tel.

07/478-3485) is on the northwest part of the main island, which has a pier, bungalow accommodations, and campgrounds.

Many people visit these islands on chartered tours from the mainland. These tours are generally done on speedboats and include lunch, a chance to enjoy the scenery, and some snorkeling.

The largest island, Ko Tarutao, is a mountainous, forested island with limestone cliffs, mangrove swamps, and white-sand beaches. The island formerly housed a detainment center for political and other prisoners, but these days it's home to some of the national park facilities as well as the biggest selection of bungalows and resorts. If you're interested in seeing the darker side of the country's history, you can visit the old prisons at Talo Udang Bay in the southernmost part of the island and Talowao Bay in the southeastern part of the island. They're connected by a trail that was built by prisoners before the site was abandoned during World War II.

Mu Ko Adang Rawi comprises two islands, Ko Adang and Ko Rawi, both characterized by light-sand beaches, verdant interiors with limestone cliffs, and some coral reefs offshore that can be easily viewed when snorkeling or diving. Many people visit these islands as part of a day trip, but if you want to stay overnight, there are some bungalows available through the parks department, or you can rent a tent from them or bring your own to camp on the beach.

Ko Kai and Ko Klang in the center of the marine park are also both popular spots for snorkeling and hanging out on the clean sandy beaches. There are no accommodations here, and tour groups will often add these islands to a multiple-island day tour.

On the larger islands, there are a small number of decent accommodations, if you are looking to hang out in the area for a few days as you island-hop from one sight to the other. If you're on a budget or really want to enjoy the natural environment unfettered by modern distractions, try camping at one of the many campgrounds or renting a bungalow from the

national parks department. The bungalows and dormitory-style rooms are basic, with running water and fan cooling, and are located on Ko Taratao. There is also a campground on the beach on both Ko Taratao and smaller Ko Adang. Prices are 500-1,500 baht per night. Book accommodations with the Department of National Parks (tel. 02/562-0760, np_income@dnp.go.th). Once the reservation is booked, you must transfer full payment to the National Parks by bank wire (or at a Krung Thai Bank or ATM in Thailand). There is a canteen at the park headquarters and another on smaller Adang Island to the west.

Ko Li Pe
เกาะหลีเป๊ะ

Just below the national park is Ko Li Pe, a small, charming island just 40 kilometers (25 mi) from Malaysia's Langkawi Island. Populated by sea gypsies and a smattering of unpretentious resorts and bungalows, every year the island is becoming more popular with adventurous vacationers looking for something a little off the beaten path. Still, it's small enough that you can tour the whole island in two hours, and you won't find any big partying or even ATMs on Ko Li Pe, just a handful of beautiful beaches and some dive shops catering to those who want to enjoy the underwater life around the island.

There are three beaches on Ko Li Pe, which is shaped roughly like a boomerang pointing northeast. The eastern beach is called Sunset Beach, the northern beach is Sunrise Beach, and the southwestern beach (the inside of the boomerang) is called Pattaya Beach. Sunrise Beach and Pattaya Beach are connected to each other by a road that functions as the island's main street.

Many resorts close up shop during low season, but there are some that remain open year-round. Idyllic Concept Resort (Sunrise Beach, tel. 08/8227-5389, www.idyllicresort.com, 3,500B) features modern, funky guest rooms and bungalows right on the beach, plus a resort restaurant. The resort opened in 2013 and is very clean and well-maintained.

Sita Beach Resort and Spa Villa (Pattaya Beach, tel. 07/475-0382, www.sitabeachresort.com, 3,500B) is a full-service midrange resort with a swimming pool, a restaurant, a bar, and a small spa. Guest rooms are comfortable and have flat-screen TVs and vaguely Thai decor. The pool area is spacious and surrounded by guest rooms and villas. The resort is very family-friendly, too. The location and the view of the beach, though, are the big attractions here.

The cool, popular, and ecochic Castaway Resort (Sunrise Beach, tel. 08/3138-7472, www.castaway-resorts.com, 2,000B) is a collection of stand-alone bamboo bungalows on the beach, plus an outdoor bar and restaurant. The accommodations are basic—there's no air-conditioning or hot water, although because the bungalows are right off the water, ceiling fans keep everything cool enough. Most bungalows have an upstairs and a downstairs plus a small balcony for lounging and enjoying the view.

MAP SYMBOLS

▭▭▭ Expressway	○ City/Town	✈ Airport	⚑ Golf Course
▭ Primary Road	◉ State Capital	✈ Airfield	▯ Parking Area
▭ Secondary Road	✷ National Capital	▲ Mountain	▲ Archaeological Site
...... Unpaved Road	★ Point of Interest	✦ Unique Natural Feature	▮ Church
—— Feature Trail	• Accommodation		⛽ Gas Station
- - - Other Trail	▼ Restaurant/Bar	⌣ Waterfall	⬭ Glacier
········ Ferry	■ Other Location	⬆ Park	▦ Mangrove
▭ Pedestrian Walkway	Λ Campground	▯ Trailhead	Reef
⬚⬚⬚ Stairs		✗ Skiing Area	▭ Swamp

CONVERSION TABLES

°C = (°F - 32) / 1.8
°F = (°C x 1.8) + 32
1 inch = 2.54 centimeters (cm)
1 foot = 0.304 meters (m)
1 yard = 0.914 meters
1 mile = 1.6093 kilometers (km)
1 km = 0.6214 miles
1 fathom = 1.8288 m
1 chain = 20.1168 m
1 furlong = 201.168 m
1 acre = 0.4047 hectares
1 sq km = 100 hectares
1 sq mile = 2.59 square km
1 ounce = 28.35 grams
1 pound = 0.4536 kilograms
1 short ton = 0.90718 metric ton
1 short ton = 2,000 pounds
1 long ton = 1.016 metric tons
1 long ton = 2,240 pounds
1 metric ton = 1,000 kilograms
1 quart = 0.94635 liters
1 US gallon = 3.7854 liters
1 Imperial gallon = 4.5459 liters
1 nautical mile = 1.852 km

°FAHRENHEIT / °CELSIUS thermometer and 24-hour clock face

°FAHRENHEIT	°CELSIUS	
230	110	
220	100	WATER BOILS
210	100	
200	90	
190	80	
180	80	
170	70	
160	70	
150	60	
140	60	
130	50	
120	50	
110	40	
100	40	
90	30	
80	30	
70	20	
60	10	
50	10	
40	0	WATER FREEZES
30	0	
20	-10	
10	-20	
0	-20	
-10	-30	
-20	-30	
-30	-40	
-40	-40	

INCH 0 1 2 3 4

CM 0 1 2 3 4 5 6 7 8 9 10

**MOON SPOTLIGHT PHUKET
& THE ANDAMAN COAST**
Avalon Travel
a member of the Perseus Books Group
1700 Fourth Street
Berkeley, CA 94710, USA
www.moon.com

Editor: Leah Gordon
Series Manager: Kathryn Ettinger
Copy Editor: Alissa Cyphers
Graphics Coordinator: Darren Alessi
Production Coordinator: Darren Alessi
Cover Design: Faceout Studios, Charles Brock
Moon Logo: Tim McGrath
Map Editor: Albert Angulo
Cartographers: Albert Angulo,
  Stephanie Poulain

ISBN-13: 978-1-61238-948-6

Text © 2015 by Suzanne Nam.
Maps © 2015 by Avalon Travel.
All rights reserved.

Printed in the United States

ABOUT THE AUTHOR

Suzanne Nam

Suzanne Nam moved to Thailand in 2005 for a one-year stint as a newspaper reporter – and she hasn't left since. Like all meaningful things, Suzanne's career was more a product of evolution than of planning: She grew up in Cambridge, Massachusetts, went to law school after college, and practiced law for five years – enough time to produce a rain forest's worth of corporate paperwork – and then she gave it all up to work toward a journalism degree at Columbia.

Next the world pulled Suzanne east – first to London, then the Middle East, and finally Bangkok. She is now a reporter for *Forbes* magazine and a dedicated travel writer.

Suzanne met her future husband during her first year in Bangkok. In 2009 they adopted a street dog named Sam; in 2011 their twins, Bix and Ella, were born. Raising children in a foreign country brings plenty of adventure and challenges, but daily life in Thailand is surprisingly stable and comfortable. Suzanne couldn't imagine living anywhere else.

CPSIA information can be obtained at www.ICGtesting.com
Printed in the USA
LVOW01s1338260315

432128LV00004B/9/P